How to Be Yourself in a World That's Different

D0104378

of related interest

Survival Strategies for People on the Autism Spectrum
Marc Fleisher
ISBN-13: 978 184310 261 8   ISBN-10: 1 84310 261 7

Freaks, Geeks and Asperger Syndrome
A User Guide to Adolescence
Luke Jackson
Foreword by Tony Attwood
ISBN-13: 978 1 84310 098 0   ISBN-10: 1 84310 098 3

Build Your Own Life
A Self-Help Guide For Individuals With Asperger Syndrome
Wendy Lawson
ISBN-13: 978 184310 114 7   ISBN-10: 1 84310 114 9

Finding Out About Asperger Syndrome, High-Functioning
Autism and PDD
Gunilla Gerland
ISBN-13: 978 185302 840 3   ISBN-10: 1 85302 840 1

Talking Teenagers
Information and Inspiration for Parents of Teenagers with
Autism or Asperger's Syndrome
Ann Boushéy
ISBN-13: 978 1 84310 844 3   ISBN-10: 1 84310 844 5

Help for the Child with Asperger's Syndrome
A Parent's Guide to Negotiating the Social Service Maze
Gretchen Mertz
ISBN-13: 978 184310 780 4   ISBN-10: 1 84310 780 5

An Asperger Dictionary of Everyday Expressions
Second Edition
Ian Stuart-Hamilton
ISBN-13: 978 1 84310 518 3   ISBN-10: 1 84310 518 7

How to Be Yourself in a World That's Different

An Asperger Syndrome Study Guide for Adolescents

Yuko Yoshida, M.D.

General Editor: Lorna Wing
Foreword by Lorna Wing

Translated by Esther Sanders

Jessica Kingsley Publishers
London and Philadelphia

First published in 2007
by Jessica Kingsley Publishers
116 Pentonville Road
London N1 9JB, UK
and
400 Market Street, Suite 400
Philadelphia, PA 19106, USA

www.jkp.com

Copyright © Institute of PsychoEducation for Children 2005
English-language text copyright © Esther Sanders 2007
Illustrations copyright © Jun'ichi Sato 2005
Foreword copyright © Lorna Wing 2007
English-language rights arranged with Institute of PsychoEducation for Children through
Spectrum Publishing Company, Tokyo
Text on p.94–5 (In the US) copyright © James McPartland 2007
Text on p.95–7 (In the UK) copyright © Lorna Wing 2007
Text on p.97–8 (In Australia) copyright © Sue Larkey 2007

Library of Congress Cataloging in Publication Data
A CIP catalog record for this book is available from the Library of Congress

British Library Cataloguing in Publication Data
A CIP catalogue record for this book is available from the British Library

ISBN-13: 978 1 84310 504 6
ISBN-10: 1 84310 504 7

Printed and bound in Great Britain by
Athenaeum Press, Gateshead, Tyne and Wear

Contents

Foreword

It was a great pleasure for me to be asked to read and edit the draft text of this book. It was translated into English – I have to confess that, sadly, I cannot read Japanese.

As soon as I started to read, it was plain to me that the author knew and understood the way in which people with Asperger syndrome experience the world. This understanding is essential for anyone wanting to convey information and encouragement to those who have the syndrome. The book begins with a clear explanation of the neurology that underlies what is special about Asperger's syndrome. It then goes on to discuss, in detail, the problems people with the syndrome experience in everyday life, giving sensible, specific suggestions for coping, with lots of practical examples.

One of the best things about the book is the way Yuko Yoshida emphasizes the many really positive aspects of the syndrome, as well as writing plainly and honestly about the difficulties. My favorite story from the book concerns a girl whose intense curiosity and search for knowledge made her ask questions that were socially unacceptable in a situation where others were concerned only with sad thoughts and feelings. Later, the girl blamed herself for her own lack of feeling, but Yuko told her, "You have the heart of a true scientist." This is a wonderful way of conveying the nature of this special way of seeing the world.

The book will be a support and comfort as well as a guide for adolescents (and for adults of any age) who have Asperger syndrome. I am sure Asperger himself would have approved of the commonsense approach of the author.

Lorna Wing

Acknowledgments

First and foremost, I wish to express my immeasurable gratitude to Dr. Lorna Wing. I am deeply grateful to her not only for so carefully scrutinizing the manuscript, but also for offering me such warm guidance and for believing that my opinions as a child psychiatrist were worthy of her consideration despite my being a generation younger and from a culture half a world away.

In addition, I would like to take this opportunity to thank the following individuals:

Dr. Tokio Uchiyama, director of Yokohama Psycho-Developmental Clinic and professor in human relations at Otsuma Women's University, and Dr. Hiroshi Fujioka, director of Tsubasa Psycho-Developmental Clinic, for their constant encouragement and useful advice.

Dr. Shinichiro Kado and Dr. Yoko Muramatsu, of the Kyoto City Child Welfare Center, for putting the material in this book to the test in their clinical practice and then offering me valuable suggestions based on what they found.

All of the clients and staff at Yokohama Psycho-Developmental Clinic, for their feedback, both direct and indirect.

Esther Sanders, for serving as a conduit for communication between myself and Dr. Wing with her faithful translations of the manuscript and correspondence.

Junichi Sato, the book's illustrator, for accomplishing the great feat of bearing with my obsessive personality to the very end.

My son, for offering me encouragement and for becoming the manuscript's first reader by means of constantly peering over my shoulder as I sat at the computer, and my husband, for being the manuscript's final reviewer and for never failing to keep his criticisms constructive.

And you – all of you who are taking the time to read this book from cover to cover.

Yuko Yoshida

How to Use This Book

THIS BOOK WILL HELP YOU LEARN ABOUT ASPERGER SYNDROME

If you have Asperger syndrome (AS), it means you have the type of brain that lets you get very enthusiastic about and deeply absorbed in things that interest you, and it means you have a wonderful kind of uniqueness. At the same time, having this type of brain tends to cause you difficulties in your relationships with other people.

The brains of people with AS are not diseased, and they are not "bad" or defective. There are plenty of individuals with AS and similar conditions who are highly accomplished in a variety of careers – as researchers, artists, skilled crafts-people, hard-working company employees, and so on. Later, in Chapter 2, I present a detailed description of the characteristics that define AS.

THIS BOOK IS NOT INTENDED TO TELL YOU WHETHER OR NOT YOU HAVE AS

Even if the characteristics you read about in this book seem to apply to you or someone you know, the cause of those characteristics might be something other than AS. Determining whether or not someone has AS requires a consultation with a professional.

IF YOU'VE BEEN TOLD YOU HAVE ANY OF THE FOLLOWING CONDITIONS, THEN THIS BOOK IS FOR YOU

This book was written primarily for children who have been diagnosed with a condition called Asperger syndrome. (A "diagnosis" simply means a medical classification of an individual according to certain of his or her characteristics.) Children who have been diagnosed with autism, however, will also benefit from using this book. "Autism" is a diagnosis given to people who share characteristics in common with AS, but show these characteristics in a more distinct way.

AS and autism together form what is called the "autistic spectrum." So the information in this book also applies to children who have been given any diagnosis that could be considered to be on the autistic spectrum.

In referring to this spectrum, medical professionals use a variety of labels: pervasive developmental disorder is one broad category, and then there are more specific terms like pervasive developmental disorder, not otherwise specified; Asperger disorder, autistic disorder, atypical autism, and so on. Research concerning AS and autism is still fairly new and has a long way to go, so experts have not yet reached wide agreement about which terms should be considered standard. This is confusing for patients and other nonexperts, so I have created the following list for you to refer to:

* Asperger syndrome (AS)

* autism

* high-functioning autism

* autistic spectrum disorder

* pervasive developmental disorder (PDD)

* pervasive developmental disorder, not otherwise specified (PDD-NOS)

* Asperger disorder

* autistic disorder

* atypical autism.

If you have been diagnosed with any of the above conditions, then this book should be of help to you.

The relationships between and among these various diagnoses is too complicated to explain briefly, and in fact such an explanation is outside the purpose of this book. I encourage you to talk with your doctor if you have any questions or doubts about the diagnosis you've been given.

THIS BOOK CAN HELP YOU CHANGE THE COURSE OF YOUR LIFE

AS characteristics are among your most important personal strengths. They are a valuable part of your individuality – an important part of who you are. At the same time, these characteristics can also be the cause of difficulties in your everyday life. I assure you, however, that there are strategies you can use to make things easier.

If this book can help you to live your life in your own way, and to do so with pride, joy, and inner peace, then my greatest hope in writing it will have been fulfilled. The first step toward changing your life in this way is for you to become more informed about AS. Knowledge is power.

FOR OPTIMUM RESULTS, I RECOMMEND SHARING THIS BOOK WITH A SUPPORT PERSON

As you read this book, please keep in mind that everything I say about AS and the autistic spectrum applies equally well to any of the other diagnostic labels listed above. But also remember that all individuals are different, so even if you've been given one of these diagnoses, chances are that not absolutely everything in this book will fit you exactly. Any self-help strategy that you use will have to be "fine-tuned" (i.e., carefully adjusted) to suit you.

So which parts of what you read on the following pages actually fit you, and which of the strategies I describe will you find helpful? It is precisely these questions that I hope you will discuss with a "support person"* – my name for any adult who is on your side and in a position to help you. (If you're uncertain about whether or not a certain person in your life would be an appropriate support person, see Chapter 6.)

---

*   Support people might include your mother, father, doctor, psychologist, or speech or language therapist, just to list a few examples.

PART I

Information

CHAPTER 1

Research Related to Asperger Syndrome

BRAIN STUDIES

In the past, medical researchers concentrated mainly on comparing the physical shape of the brains of people with and without AS. No clear differences in shape were found, however. Recently, a new line of inquiry has produced some clear answers: there has been some research showing that people with AS and those without it use different parts of their brains to think and solve problems. (In this book, I will be using the term "the majority" to refer to people who are not on the autistic spectrum.)

On the following pages, I present the results of two related research studies published in recent years, one led by Dr. Robert Schultz (Schultz *et al.* 2000) and another led by Dr. Simon Baron-Cohen (Baron-Cohen *et al.* 1999).

Study 1: Schultz *et al.* (2000)

In each of the four boxes below is a pair of photos. Schultz and his colleagues asked subjects (participants in their study) to look at each pair and guess whether or not both photos were of the same person or object. Fourteen of the subjects were on the autistic spectrum, and 28 were people in the majority. While the subjects were looking at the pictures and thinking, the researchers determined which parts of their brains were being used. (The correct answers are as follows: Box A shows two different people; Box B shows the same person twice; Box C shows two different objects; and Box D shows the same object twice.)

The same, or different?

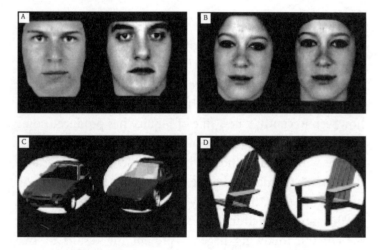

Results

The red and yellow areas below are the areas of the brain that subjects were using when they looked at the photos and thought about each question.

First, take a look at the top row. The green frames show the parts of the brain used by people in the majority in situations A (when looking at people's faces) and B (when looking at objects).

What about people on the autistic spectrum (bottom row)? When these subjects worked on the task of distinguishing faces, they hardly used those parts of the brain at all. Instead, they used much the same part of the brain used by majority subjects to distinguish between objects.

So here we have clear evidence that people with and without AS have different types of brains. Moreover, the

When looking at
people's faces

When looking
at objects

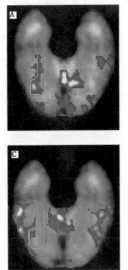

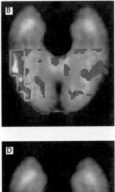

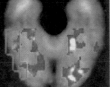

study provides evidence that this difference is responsible for the difficulty that individuals with AS often have remembering people's faces and distinguishing between two people who look similar.

Study 2: Baron-Cohen *et al.* (1999)

This study included six subjects on the autistic spectrum and 12 in the majority. The researchers showed subjects photos like the one below and asked them to guess the emotions of the people in the photos by looking at their eyes. The researchers then determined which parts of the brain subjects were using while doing this task.

Is the person in this photo concerned, or unconcerned?

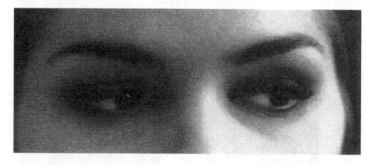

The correct answer is that the person in the photo is concerned.

Results

As we did with Study 1, let's use colored frames to analyze the results. When attempting to guess what the person in the photograph was feeling by looking at the eyes, people in the majority used the parts of the brain shown in yellow and blue. Meanwhile, people on the autistic spectrum also used the parts of the brain shown in blue, but not those shown in yellow; instead, they used the parts of the brain shown in red (not used by majority subjects).

Cross-sections from the bottom portion of the brain...

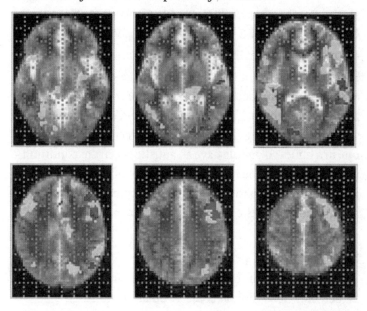

...to the top portion of the brain

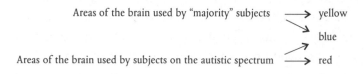

Areas of the brain used by "majority" subjects ⟶ yellow

↘ blue

↗

Areas of the brain used by subjects on the autistic spectrum ⟶ red

This research study provides further evidence that people with AS use different parts of the brain from people in the majority when solving the same problem.

HOW COMMON IS THE TYPE OF BRAIN THAT CHARACTERIZES THE AUTISTIC SPECTRUM?

People with AS are in the minority

Studies have shown that the percentage of people on the autistic spectrum (people with any of the conditions listed on pp.11–12) is about 1 percent of the world's total population, with results ranging from 0.9 to 1.2 percent. In other words, one in a hundred people have an autistic spectrum condition – many fewer than the number of people who don't. This is my reason for referring to those on the spectrum as "the minority" and to the rest of the population as "the majority."

So how many is 1 percent?

To get an idea of how many people are represented by "1 percent," let's look at some population statistics.

The world's population is currently about 5.9 billion (5,901,000,000). Of this number, about 126 million (126,070,000), or 2.1 percent, are Japanese. And about 58.7 million (58,650,000), or 1 percent, are from the UK. So there are about as many people in the world with an autistic spectrum condition as the total number of people living in the UK.

But let's look at one more interesting statistic, just to widen our perspective. Sweden's population is about 8.9 million (8,850,000), or 0.15 percent of the world's population. Hmm... This means that being born in the land of the Nobel Prize is much rarer than being born with an autistic spectrum condition.

Various groups as percentages of world's population

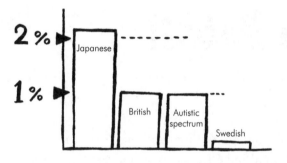

I imagine that there are very few children or teenagers in Japan who have never seen a person from the UK, even if only through catching glimpses of Queen Elizabeth II on the evening news or watching Daniel Radcliffe star in the Harry Potter movies. Similarly, I suspect that very few people in Japan, or anywhere for that matter, have never met a person who is on the autistic spectrum. But you cannot tell whether someone is on the spectrum just by looking, so you might easily meet such a person and not know it. To describe "1 percent" in another way: the number is small enough so that you probably would not come across a person in this category if you specifically went out looking, but large enough so that you might meet one in passing without ever realizing it.

CHAPTER 2

Asperger Syndrome in Detail

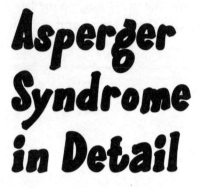

The following outline will make it easier for you to understand and organize what you're going to learn about AS in this chapter.

The triad – three sets of characteristics shared by everyone who has AS:

* characteristics of socialization (interpersonal relations)

* characteristics of communication

* characteristics of imagination (including mental shifting – by which I mean changing one's mood or the focus of one's attention – and generalizing about ideas and information).

Non-triad characteristics that are shared by many, but not all, people with AS:

* unusual qualities of sensory perception

* difficulties with sports and with movement in general.

Other brain types that often coexist with AS:

* attention deficit/hyperactivity disorder (AD/HD)

* learning disorders (LDs)

* tics.

TRIAD CHARACTERISTICS
Socialization (interpersonal relations)

Below are some examples of the ways in which the social characteristics of AS are often manifested. These traits can sometimes be a source of difficulty, but at the same time they are also valuable, positive human attributes.

Some common advantages of having autistic spectrum social traits

* Unique ideas that would never occur to people bound by so-called common sense (this is also a characteristic of imagination)

* A strong inclination to take rules seriously, even those that the majority tend to take lightly or ignore

* A tendency to be unbiased in the sense of not judging others by their age or social status

* A strong sense of equality and justice, and strong feelings for groups of people in any part of the world being treated badly, even if none are known personally

* Loyalty to one's friends

* A tendency to be very kind and gentle
* The determination to follow one's plans to completion and to do things in one's own way
* A knack for enjoying time spent alone.

Some of the disadvantages

* A tendency to be told, "You need more common sense!"
* Trouble related to the inability to understand what people are thinking or feeling
* Difficulty making friends and getting along with people
* A tendency to get left out or shunted aside despite trying hard to be liked.

Note: Please remember that while everyone with AS has socialization distortions, they won't all share these specific examples.

Communication

People with AS have many difficulties with conversation, but in fact also have many strengths in the area of language.

Common advantages of having autistic spectrum communication traits

* Pleasure in using words accurately
* Pleasure in conveying facts, such as dates and numerical information, accurately

* A strong interest in, and wide knowledge of, sophisticated vocabulary and technical terminology

* A tendency to be good at memorizing passages of writing that are of personal interest

* A unique and interesting way of expressing oneself

* A tendency to be especially good at thinking up puns

* A sincere respect for language and desire to become even better at speaking and listening

* A tendency to be highly diligent, with a background that includes having learned to converse despite numerous communication difficulties.

Some of the disadvantages

* Difficulty conveying one's own thoughts with words and a tendency to be misunderstood

* A tendency to make conversation that is considered by others to be tedious, hard to understand, or one-sided

* Occasional difficulty understanding what one hears during a conversation; understanding each individual word but having trouble piecing them together

* Perplexity at the fact that everyone but oneself seems to understand idioms that contain metaphors (such as the expression "put your best foot forward" to mean "try your best" or "show off your best qualities")

* Occasional bizarre misunderstandings that leave others flabbergasted

* A frequent tendency to have trouble using body language (facial expressions, gaze, gestures, etc.) appropriately and to lack awareness of the use of body language by others

* A frequent tendency to be left out of conversations, for reasons that are difficult to discern.

Note: Please remember that these are only examples and that not all of them apply to every person who has AS.

Imagination

Some situations require the use of imagination; the ability to generalize (to apply ideas or information we've learned before to a new but similar situation); or the ability to make mental shifts – for example, to adjust our moods and the focus of our attention when something unexpected happens. All of these skills are related in the sense that they involve dealing with things that we can't actually see. The AS characteristics of imagination (including mental shifts and generalizing) have the hidden potential to add extraordinary richness to your life in many ways. But if you live your life without being aware of these characteristics, these advantages can easily turn into disadvantages. Your awareness is vital!

Some of the common advantages of having autistic spectrum imagination traits

* Unique ideas that would never occur to people bound by so-called common sense (this is also a characteristic of socialization)

* Interests that are "narrow and deep," not "wide and shallow"

* More eagerness and thoroughness than most other people about pursuing things of interest

* A great thirst for knowledge and a talent for researching and learning new things

* An ability to get absorbed in reading books on subjects of personal interest, even when they are reference books such as atlases or dictionaries

* In some cases, enthusiasm about building collections of items related to a special interest

* The power to accomplish goals in areas one enjoys or has decided are worthwhile

* A feeling of security and an ability to perform well and fulfill one's potential when expectations are clear

* An appreciation for the importance of discipline in following established procedures

* In many cases, an appreciation for the value of following rules

* A very good memory for things or processes of interest

* The ability to enjoy one's own imaginary world and use this as a means of relaxing or refueling one's energy.

Some of the disadvantages

* ★ Problems resulting from a strong need to do certain things or have things done a certain way
* ★ Trouble switching from one activity or thought pattern to another
* ★ Difficulty generalizing
* ★ Presumptions (ideas about what things are or what they should be) that are sometimes too strong
* ★ A tendency to get upset when anything is different from usual or from what one had expected
* ★ Trouble predicting possible outcomes before actually doing something (especially when trying something new or guessing what another person will think)
* ★ Occasionally, trouble grasping what is interesting about novels or fictional television shows, such as soap operas or situation comedies
* ★ A tendency to get deeply absorbed in one's own fantasy world.

Note: Please remember that these are only examples and that not all of them apply to every person who has AS.

The triad characteristics do not always show themselves to the same degree

At the beginning of a new school term, the anxiety you feel may make it more difficult than usual for you to be flexible about your habits or put aside your preoccupations. And whenever you're feeling tense, it might be harder than usual for you to understand what people are saying to you. These changes are not uncommon. Anxiety, tension, and psychological fatigue can all make the triad characteristics show themselves as difficulties rather than strengths.

But the reverse is also true. Reducing anxiety and stress, and organizing your life so as to avoid fatigue, will help prevent the triad characteristics from being manifested as weaknesses. There are also numerous other strategies that you can develop to prevent this and to instead enable your triad characteristics to shine through as strengths. I will be talking about these kinds of strategies a great deal in Part 2.

NON-TRIAD CHARACTERISTICS
Auditory hypersensitivity

"Auditory hypersensitivity" means problems related to hearing that involve being strongly attuned to sound (but without actually having a problem with the power of hearing itself).

Sounds are "heard" with the brain

Sound results from vibrations in the air (sound waves). Sound waves hit the eardrum (tympanic membrane) and cause it to vibrate. This vibration is transmitted to the inner ear and changed into an electrical impulse, which is picked up by the auditory nerve and carried to the brain. The brain analyzes the electrical impulse and defines it as "so much sound," "this kind of tone," "just like the sound I heard at such and such a time in the past," etc. In other words, "sound" is not what we hear with our ears, but rather what we recognize with our brains.

People with AS often have atypical responses to sound

Very frequently, people with AS respond to sound differently than the majority of the general population. This seems only

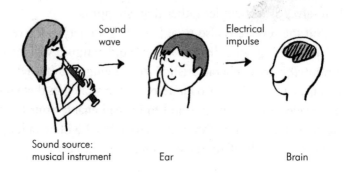

Sound source:
musical instrument   Ear   Brain

natural, since the brains of people on the autistic spectrum are different from the brains of most people, and, as discussed above, the brain is ultimately what we use to "hear," or recognize, sound.

Some people with AS are lucky enough to have unusual skills, such as perfect pitch or the ability to make subtle distinctions between similar sounds. At the same time, some people with AS have to cope with the difficulty of being hypersensitive in their responses to sound. For example, even things like a little bit of static, which people in the majority can simply ignore, are highly intrusive to people with auditory hypersensitivity and can be extremely distressful and distracting.

The severity of auditory hypersensitivity varies depending on the circumstances

The brain's ability to recognize sound without difficulty can change, depending on the person's physical condition and level of stress at any given moment. Auditory hypersensitivity does not occur simply because a person comes into contact with a very loud noise or a noise of the sort they find particularly bothersome. It also tends to get worse as a result of feeling especially anxious or tense, being fatigued, or being spoken to by several people at the same time.

Looking at the positive side, this means that you can reduce problems resulting from auditory hypersensitivity by reducing anxiety and tension and by taking good care of your body, as well as by avoiding excessively loud noises or environments where too many sources of sound can be heard at once.

Other sensory distortions

People with AS can experience distortions, or imbalances, in senses other than hearing. Some people with AS have a number of different sensory distortions, while others have hardly any problem in this area at all. Some individuals may have had sensory problems as young children that they have now outgrown. Below, I describe some of the other types of distortions, aside from those related to hearing, that often occur.

Tactile sense distortions

The tactile sense – the sense of touch involving the hands, the skin (including both the face and other parts of the body), the inside of the mouth, etc. – can be distorted in various ways:

* A strong desire to stroke objects that are soft and fluffy or smooth and slippery, or to hold them up to one's cheek

* A habit of putting pencils or other objects in one's mouth or holding them up to the lips without thinking about it

* A feeling of relaxation when kneading things with one's fingertips or grasping objects that feel squishy

* In contrast, difficulty experiencing certain sensations (e.g., the feel of squishy or rough objects on one's fingers or other parts of the skin; the feel of scratchy clothing, which may be unbearable; the texture of certain foods, such as those that are pasty or gooey)

* A great aversion to being touched by other people, especially when it happens suddenly.

Distortions in the sense of pressure

* A feeling of relaxation from the feeling of having one's body squeezed or pressed, for example by being wrapped up tightly in a cotton blanket

* In contrast, a complete inability to tolerate sensations like these.

Visual sense distortions

Here we have individual differences in the way people look at objects or the things they like to look at, unrelated to acuity of eyesight:

* Special pleasure in the physical act of looking at objects and, in particular, viewing them from a variety of angles

* A strong desire to look at specific types of objects, or an inability to stop looking at them (e.g., things that are round, that spin, that are shiny, or that are of a certain color)

* An extreme aversion to bright light.

Olfactory sense distortions

Hypersensitivity or hyposensitivity to smells:

* Frequent awareness of odors that other people don't notice, or an inability to tolerate being around certain smells

* An unusually good memory for smells, or an ability to make subtle distinctions between different smells

* Difficulty noticing smells.

Gustatory sense distortions

Imbalances in the way one perceives taste:

* An inability to tolerate certain tastes, even ones that most people love

* A desire to eat things with the same type of flavor all the time

* Enjoyment since early childhood of foods with bitter or sour tastes, or other tastes usually enjoyed only by adults (e.g., coffee without sugar, blue cheese, raw onions, or pickled fish).

Distortions in the sense of pain

Imbalances in the way one experiences pain:

* A very high threshold for pain

* In contrast, an extreme sensitivity to certain types of pain, to a degree that others consider to be exaggerated (whether or not one has a high threshold for pain in general).

Distortions in the sense of balance (vestibular sense)

Imbalances in the way one feels when spinning or experiencing upward or downward motion:

* A tendency to get motion sickness very easily

* A special enjoyment, in contrast, of the rocking sensation felt when riding in a car or on a train

* An ability to spin in circles without getting dizzy; a desire to spin in circles as a solitary activity

* A preference (either now or as a young child) for riding on swings or in elevators, being lifted high in the air, or activities providing similar sensations.

The severity of sensory distortions varies depending on the circumstances

Just as with auditory hypersensitivity, distortions or imbalances in other senses can vary, depending on how secure or relaxed you are feeling at a given time, what kind of physical shape you're in, or other circumstances. And, just as with noise in the environment, there are definitely strategies you can develop to reduce the amount of discomfort you experience as a result of these atypical sensory characteristics.

Difficulties with sports, and with movement in general

Many people with AS have difficulties involving the use of their bodies. For example:

* they are sometimes told that they have an unusual way of walking, or they may have a tendency to be unsteady on their feet or to fall easily

* they are not good at sports (or, like a small number of people with AS, they are extraordinary good at certain sports)

* they have a tendency to bump into things when they walk, to drop things, or to graze one object against

another (e.g., hitting a plate that they are putting away against the edge of the cupboard)

* they often spill when eating or drinking
* they are "all thumbs" – i.e., clumsy with their hands.

Being clumsy or poor at sports is the sort of thing that is likely to get you teased; for this and other reasons, it can be very, very stressful. But when you reach adulthood and are out on your own, you will be able to choose the kinds of physical activities you engage in and also to what extent and in what way you pursue these activities. You will be free to say to yourself, for example, "I will get all of my exercise from walking and never play sports again!" and then to live your life accordingly.

So, basically, all of the bad experiences associated with sports and physical activity can be put behind you once you are out of school. And in the meantime, there are probably things you can do, with the help of a support person, to reduce the number of these bad experiences or to make them less of a burden.

OTHER TYPES OF BRAIN

There's more to brain type than just "AS" versus "Not AS"

There are other types of brain aside from the autistic spectrum type. For example, there are brain characteristics that determine whether you are left-handed or right-handed, or left-eye dominant or right-eye dominant (i.e., whether you look through camera viewfinders and such with your left or right eye). Determining your brain subtype (i.e., the combination of all the different types that describe you) is not a simple, one-step process. Take a look at the chart on page 38, and you'll see what I mean. Let's examine three other brain types that often coexist with the autistic spectrum type in the same individual.

Flow chart illustrating the determination of brain type

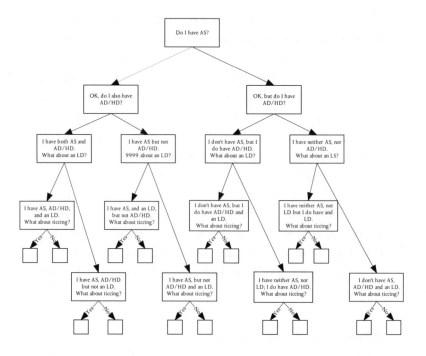

Aside from all the different possibilities lined up above, there are still other brain sub-types (i.e., combinations). For example, left-handedness and right-handedness are two other brain types. Which box above do you think might give the best description of your brain subtype? Try comparing brain types with your support person.

Attention deficit/hyperactivity disorder (AD/HD)
What is AD/HD?
Having AD/HD means having symptoms of inattention or of hyperactivity and impulsivity, or of both, to a degree that causes you problems in your daily life.

Symptoms of inattention:

* Making frequent careless mistakes in arithmetic or other subjects

* Often forgetting or losing things

* Becoming oblivious to everything else when absorbed in an activity and possibly even being spoken to without noticing

* Being easily distractible, especially with activities that are not of interest or that require patience

* Tuning out or daydreaming at a time when concentration is required

* Having difficulty keeping one's belongings organized

* Forgetting to do routine things that for most people come as second nature (e.g., forgetting to hand in homework, keep shirttails tucked in, or close the door to the bathroom).

Symptoms of hyperactivity and impulsivity:

* Being restless

* Often moving some part of the body even while seated in class (e.g., jiggling legs or fidgeting with the hands)

* Being unable to stop talking while everyone is supposed to be listening to the teacher

* Frequently doing things on a whim and being told, "You need to think before you act!"

Having an AD/HD-type brain is very common

Experts now believe that more than 8 percent of the general population (i.e., one in every 12 people) has AD/HD, making the condition quite common. It is far more common among the population of individuals who have AS. A colleague and I conducted a study and found that 60.4 percent of subjects with ASD also had symptoms of inattention (Yoshida and Uchiyama 2004).

People with AD/HD are full of energy and have the potential to get a lot done. Just as with the characteristics of AS, once you develop a knack for harnessing the tremendous energy that comes with AD/HD, this condition can become a driving force in your life that will enable you to profit in many ways.

Learning disorders (LDs)

Asperger pointed out that some people with AS have one or more specific learning disorders (LDs) despite having an overall level of intelligence in the average or even superior range (Asperger 1944 [1991]).

What are LDs?

Having an LD means that you have great difficulty with one or more of the following three areas of study, despite the fact that your IQ* is not below the level that represents normal intelligence.

---

*   IQ, which stands for "intelligence quotient," is a measure of just one small part of human ability. It is a numerical score based on a test that was developed to fit the majority way of doing things. An individual's IQ score is one indication of how easily he or she is likely to progress with schoolwork, but the score has no significance beyond this. For example, it does not determine how easily a person with AS is likely to manage in everyday life apart from school.

Difficulty with writing:

* Having problems with spelling

* Forgetting familiar letters or words after just a short break from writing them – in less time than it would take most people to forget

* Making the same mistakes repeatedly (e.g., confusing the letters *b* and *d*).

Difficulty reading either individual letters, words, or connected text:

* Not being able to remember the pronunciations of individual letters or words

* Being able to read individual letters or words but having great difficulty reading connected text fluently

* Finding it extremely difficult to comprehend meaning when reading, to an extent that cannot be explained away merely by the communication difficulties that are among the characteristics of AS.

Difficulty doing arithmetic:

* Becoming overwhelmed with confusion just from thinking about anything related to numbers

* Being unable to get a solid grasp of how to do calculations (this is separate from the issue of making careless mistakes).

People with LDs are often misunderstood, and their difficulties are thought to be due to laziness. If you have an LD, it is important for you to talk with your support person and work out a strategy that will help others understand you more accurately.

Tics

What are tics?

When a part of your body moves or a word or sound comes out of your mouth involuntarily – that is, all by itself, without you doing it deliberately – this is called a tic. The following behaviors, when they occur involuntarily, are examples of tics: excessive blinking, head turning, shoulder lifting, throat clearing, or, again, any kind of vocalization. Tics are another characteristic that is determined by brain type.

Ticcing is a symptom that often occurs in people who have AS. One group of researchers has found that about 80 percent of people with AS exhibit tics at one time or another, and, further, that 20 percent of individuals who exhibited a variety of tics over a long period of time actually had an autistic spectrum condition (Gillberg 2002).

Tics as a measure of stress level

Just as with auditory hypersensitivity and insistence on certain habits and preoccupations, tics tend to increase when a person is in a state of high anxiety, stress, or psychological fatigue. Some people actually use this phenomenon as a way of monitoring their own level of stress at any given time. In other words, when they notice that they're ticcing more, they interpret this as a psychological warning signal and talk with their support person about what the cause might be and what they can do to alleviate the problem. This is an excellent idea, since people with AS often have difficulty realizing when they are in a state of mental fatigue.

Strategies for dealing with tics

It is very common for people to be able to suppress tics temporarily (i.e., to make them stop for a short period of time) if they concentrate on this intensely to the exclusion of everything else. But doing this while in class, for example, would make it impossible to focus on what the teacher is saying, and it is also exhausting. It is not unusual for a person's ticcing to actually become worse overall as a result of constant, stress-filled efforts at suppression.

Tics can be lessened with medication. If you have tics that are conspicuous and causing you distress, then I recommend that you discuss this option with your doctor. The same drugs prescribed to reduce tics can also reduce anxiety, so in some cases, medication is effective at treating not only the tics themselves, but also their cause. But if your ticcing is the result of a high level of anxiety or stress, then your most important priority should be making adjustments to your environment – i.e., to the way your daily life is arranged. Please talk this over with your support person.

CHAPTER 3

Temporary Mental Dysfunction

Both people with AS and those without it can occasionally experience imbalances in brain chemistry leading to temporary mental states that are dysfunctional. Because of their position as a social minority, people with AS tend to have stress-filled lives, and some experts believe that they are constitutionally predisposed to chemical imbalances. Certain medications have been developed for the purpose of treating these types of dysfunctional states. Three common types of dysfunction are depressive states, anxiety, and obsessiveness and compulsiveness, which I describe below, before I look at other symptoms and strategies for dealing with these states.

TYPES OF DYSFUNCTION
Depressive states
People in a temporary depressive state cannot motivate themselves to move forward; their enthusiasm is diminished; and they demonstrate less-able judgment than they normally would. For example:

* they may cry for no apparent reason, be unable to enjoy themselves, feel lethargic, or be irritable or easily angered

* they have trouble motivating themselves to accomplish tasks, and in more severe cases may even lose the desire to work on the hobbies they are usually devoted to

* their cognitive powers (e.g., their ability to do even simple arithmetic) are temporarily diminished

* they experience sleeping difficulties: waking in the middle of the night, rising too early, or being unable to fall asleep at bed-time (or, instead, they oversleep because of mental fatigue)

* their appetites become sluggish (or, instead, they overeat because of stress)

* they may experience physical symptoms, such as headaches or abdominal pain.

Anxiety
People in a state of anxiety may experience symptoms such as the following:

* they may feel a vague sort of restlessness and insecurity with regard to their daily lives

* they may be overwhelmed by worries about some specific issue, such as war or serious illness

* they may repeatedly experience an acute condition known as a "panic attack" (the sudden onset of symptoms such as the following: (1) an unbearably strong feeling of insecurity and (2) a variety of physical symptoms, often including a racing of the

pulse, tightness of the chest, discomfort in or
difficulty with breathing, heavy perspiration or a
feeling of chilliness, trembling, nausea, or
lightheadedness).

Problems with sleep or appetite are also common in cases
where anxiety has been ongoing for some time.

Obsessiveness and compulsiveness

Obsessiveness and compulsiveness are related to anxiety.
They involve engaging in certain thought patterns or habits
to a degree that is distressing, and finding it extremely
difficult to stop. In fact, a person in this state will find it harder
to stop the more he or she tries to. People with AS ordinarily
experience some degree of inflexibility with regard to their
thoughts and habits, but the possibility that this tendency has
reached the point of temporary mental dysfunction should be
considered if the behavior has become endlessly repetitive,
causing the person engaging in it to feel conflicted.

   People in a state of obsessiveness or compulsiveness may
experience symptoms such as the following:

* they may deliberately try to suppress certain
  thoughts, and yet these very thoughts keep surfacing
  repeatedly in their minds

* they may be unable to stop themselves from
  engaging in certain behaviors (such as repeated
  hand-washing or checking over and over to see if
  the windows and doors are locked), even though
  they understand these behaviors to be unnecessary
  and a waste of time.

Slowing up of movements

A small number of people with AS, when under stress causing high anxiety, may experience difficulty with movements; for example:

* they may move much more slowly than usual

* they may find it hard to begin any movement or to finish a movement once started

* they may have difficulty walking through doors, across lines in pavements, or moving from one type of surface (e.g., a wooden floor) to another (e.g., a carpet)

* they may speak much less than usual.

Other symptoms

People may experience other symptoms, such as the following, that involve extreme hypersensitivity to their surroundings and are related to the phenomenon of temporary mental dysfunction:

* they may experience the feeling that others wish them harm and that they cannot let down their guard

* they may feel that others hate them or consider them ridiculous because of their appearance (or odor)

* they may interpret a certain sound as a bad omen and become extremely distressed as a result

* they may be distressed because they think they hear someone uttering insults even though they're in a situation where no other voices could possibly be heard

⋆ they may experience a distressing worsening of
   auditory hypersensitivity, tics, or other symptoms
   that they ordinarily have to a milder degree.

STRATEGIES FOR DEALING WITH TEMPORARY MENTAL DYSFUNCTION

When someone is physically ill, getting well usually involves
resting quietly, conserving energy, and taking appropriate
medicine. These same treatments also apply when a person's
brain chemistry has gotten out of balance.

Resting the mind

If you find yourself in a state of temporary mental dysfunction
similar to any of those described above, then you should first
of all arrange your daily schedule in a way that will help you
avoid fatigue and conserve mental energy. Being around other
people can be very tiring, so in some situations it may be
important for you to take a break from school (perhaps with a
note from your doctor) and spend more time at home.

Taking appropriate medication

I also recommend that you promptly consult a doctor and
get a prescription for appropriate medication that will help
restore your brain's chemical balance. There is no shame in
taking medication, and this is certainly the ideal solution if it
means that the imbalance can be corrected quickly. Coping
with mental dysfunction over a long period of time is a waste
of energy – energy that you can better spend on making the
most of your true self.

Early awareness

Early awareness is important, but easier said than done. When you are in a state of mental dysfunction, you may have even less awareness than usual of how you are actually feeling or behaving. I recommend that you talk with your support person as soon as you notice that you haven't been sleeping well or can't seem to relax. And if a doctor determines that you are indeed experiencing a temporary dysfunctional state, I encourage you to rest in accordance with his or her instructions. Self-awareness is actually harder than you might think.

PART 2

CHAPTER 4

Special Strategies for Coping

THE PURPOSE OF SPECIAL STRATEGIES

Here, in Part 2, let's turn our attention to the discussion of strategies. But first, I would like to make sure you know the answer to a crucial question – in fact, the most important question of all regarding this topic: Why do you need special strategies? Many people with Asperger syndrome misunderstand this issue, and they suffer as a result. The purpose of using strategies, as I hope the following stories and discussion will make clear, is simply to make your daily life easier and more pleasant.

The way you think and feel

Here's something a girl in junior high school told me:

> When I was in kindergarten, my grandmother died, and after the funeral ceremony I went with everyone to the crematorium. From that day on, I kept wondering what

temperature was required to burn a human body. Then my
grandfather died last year, and again I attended the cremation. Finally, I just had to ask someone the question that
had been on my mind all those years, so I asked my father.
My father asked someone on the staff at the crematorium
and came back to me with the answer. We were all paying
our last respects to my grandma and grandpa, who loved
me so much, and instead of feeling sad I was feeling
curious about oven temperatures. I must be a horrible
person, don't you think?

This girl's parents accepted that she had a thirst for knowledge in keeping with a person who has AS, and no one who
was with them that day criticized her. And yet, the girl had it
in her head that her feelings made her a bad person.

There is nothing at all bad about that girl. She has
the heart of a scientist. The way she valued her grandparents and her wanting to know more about the unfamiliar
cremation equipment are two separate feelings. Whoever
invented crematoriums in the first place must have been a
person with a great mind and the heart of a scientist, just like
hers. And this girl, in fact, was a gentle person with a very
decent character.

For people in the majority, the death of someone they
were close to is an occasion when scientific inquiry shuts off.
But for some people with AS, who are in the minority, this
part of their nature exists independently of the thoughts they
had for the deceased, and it continues working. If their
scientific leanings are extremely strong, it would not be at all
unusual for thoughts of the person who has died not even to
surface until after some time has passed. It is not a matter of
which group's manner of experiencing emotion is correct and
which incorrect.

Another girl, a third-grader in elementary school, once told me this: "Whenever I say the first thing that is on my mind, something unpleasant happens. So instead I always say the *second* thing that is on my mind. I can't just be myself. I have to fake it."

At the time, this girl did not know that she had AS. Nevertheless, she was aware of having a different way of thinking and feeling from most people, and she was deliberately behaving in ways that the majority would find easy to accept. What wonderful insight! What marvelous skill! Yet just when she was demonstrating this exemplary behavior, she felt sad and thought there was something wrong with her.

You're not wrong, you're just rare!

You probably experience all sorts of problems as a result of your AS traits. A life full of trouble is something you want to avoid, both for your own sake and for the sake of those around you, so you've undertaken the challenge of developing a range of new strategies and skills.

This means that you will probably try to avoid asking scientific questions at funerals and may decide to make it your firm policy only to voice thoughts that reflect the AS part of your personality in the presence of people you can trust. This is good strategic thinking!

But don't forget: The reason you need special strategies is not because your way of being is wrong, but rather to make your life easier and more pleasant. The emotional processes and behavior patterns characteristic of AS are perfectly valid. It just happens, by coincidence, that you live on a planet where you're in the minority.

You're not a faker, and you're not doing anything wrong. There's no need for you to try to think and feel the same way as the majority. When you face a crematorium with people in mourning, you do not need to abandon your sense of wonder, your curiosity about temperature, fuel sources, or whatever else. As long as you keep good strategy in mind and save your questions about these things for another time, then your thoughts and feelings are perfectly legitimate.

Again, what you need to work on is how to make your life easier. But it's not a matter of learning the "right" way; it's simply a matter of learning the majority way.

THREE PRINCIPLES FOR DEVELOPING GOOD STRATEGIES

The following three principles will help you not only to decide on good strategies, but also to implement them effectively.

Principle 1: Don't look for problems to fix, look for talents to use!

Let's take the example of hypersensitive hearing (p.31). Let's say that you are really bothered by noise, such as when lots of people are talking all at once in class, or when you have to ride the subway during rush hour or walk through crowded, busy streets. Because the brains of people with auditory hypersensitivity process sounds differently from the brains of most people, if you have this condition you might get confused when spoken to even though you would understand the same information just fine if it were written down for you. When you think about the problem this way, it does seem as though auditory hypersensitivity can put you at a definite disadvantage.

But on the other hand, your talent for discriminating between different types of sounds could provide you with a source of enjoyment. Some people have perfect pitch, and some are able to build careers using their ability to recognize subtle differences between sounds. There are famous musicians, such as the French composer Erik Satie, who were never diagnosed but are now thought to have had Asperger syndrome based on biographical information about their childhoods and the way they lived (see Gillberg 2002).

It's the same with the triad characteristics. It's not unusual for the parents of children with AS also to have some of the characteristics, but many of these adults are highly successful in their lives precisely because of these traits. For example, they feel a strong sense of responsibility regarding their professional commitments; they approach subjects that interest them with enthusiasm, great concentration, and a thirst for knowledge; they have unique ideas; and they have the determination and courage to live in accordance with their own values. Does any of this remind you of your mother or father?

AS characteristics are not enemies that need to be destroyed. They are your allies – your most important strengths.

Principle 2: Don't look for problems to fix, look for traits to complement!

Although AS traits give you valuable advantages, it is still best to have a plan for making the most of them by using strategies that complement them, and this requires effort.

For example, even if you can't change your auditory hypersensitivity, you may still be able to spend time in noisy environments if you use earplugs or a Walkman to shield yourself from sounds that make you uncomfortable. Your brain's ability to process sound is affected by anxiety and tension (see p.32–3), so one effective habit is to confirm the details of upcoming events ahead of time in order to put your mind at ease; this, in turn, will better enable you to handle unpleasant noises during the event itself. Using little tricks like these can mean less inconvenience and discomfort for you in your everyday life.

To give you another example, let's say that you have always found it hard to cope with sudden schedule changes. If you get into the habit of consistently following the plan you've input into your electronic notebook – and learn to feel at ease with this process – then you will be able to manage unavoidable changes without being upset by them. When changes occur, you can simply edit your electronic schedule and then read the new schedule over and over again until the new plan settles comfortably into your thoughts.

In Chapter 5 I introduce several specific ideas for complementing autistic spectrum characteristics. The details of each strategy, however, must be varied to fit each individual. I encourage you to discuss with your support person any particular difficulties that you are currently having. Discovering strategies to complement your natural traits is a highly worthwhile pursuit.

Principle 3: Gain experience in a planned, step-by-step manner

Some people will say that merely complementing your AS traits is not enough, that improvement in coping and life-management skills also requires lots of experience and the practice that comes with it.

I am against the idea of using haphazard experience as a way of practicing skills. I have met many children who have been forced to participate in social and communicative experiences where they endured the public embarrassment of failure after failure to the extent that they suffered psychological damage and lost all self-confidence. The emotional distress of these children is so deep that it cannot be fully expressed in words.

Those of you reading this have already made tremendous efforts. You have endured painful experiences unlike those of children in the majority. If there are things in your life that are not going well, then this is certainly not because of any need to try harder.

Of course experience is important. But experiences need to be deliberately planned so that they are accumulated in stages, step by step. If you proceed on the thinking that you need to keep loading yourself up with any and all experiences, then you will only get hurt, and your success will be hindered.

Let's look at the following stages for planning your learning experiences, which can be thought of as practice sessions.

Stage 1: Choose the right goal

There may be times when what you really need to work on (e.g., looking for satisfying ways to spend free time by yourself, or going with your support person to explore places where you're more likely to find people with common interests) is different from what you want to practice (e.g., using your free time to work on making good conversation with friends). Choosing the wrong goal will only lead you to frustration and will make it harder for you to succeed. It is very important that you get off to a good start on the process of alleviating the particular burdens that are making your life more difficult than it could be. Please talk with your support person about what goal is best for you to work toward next.

Stage 2: Start by accumulating knowledge

People with AS have a hard time sorting through lots of information to select what is important and what can be ignored. For this reason, a person with AS who has gone through a challenging experience will have difficulty evaluating the results and figuring out why he or she did poorly while the other people involved did well.

Therefore, I suggest that you start by creating a knowledge base: Before putting yourself into a challenging situation, write down as many details as possible about the skill you are planning to practice – for example, rules that will raise the chances of success, specific examples of what you should say and of things you should not do, and clues you should watch for to help you figure out how other people are reacting. I definitely think that the help of a support person is crucial for this stage.

When it comes time for the actual experience, your most important task will be judging whether and when each piece of knowledge you've accumulated is applicable; simply having the knowledge will not automatically make you successful. But having it is certainly better than not having it.

Stage 3: Work on observing and making inferences

In the midst of a social or communicative experience, you do not have a videotape that you can rewind and play back in order to evaluate what you've just said or the facial expression you've just used. And during an exchange that occurs in class, you will also feel pressured. It is therefore especially difficult to learn from this kind of immersion in direct experience.

A better way to start is by using comic strips, TV soap operas or situation comedies, or animated videos to practice making observations and inferences. Challenge yourself, as if you were participating in a quiz show, to come up with answers to questions like these: Why did a certain character respond to another in a particular way? What are the characters communicating with their facial expressions and gestures? Why did a certain character get angry? Why did another character cry, or laugh? What is interesting about the story? The purpose of this self-imposed quiz is for you to practice analyzing how people in the majority think and feel and how they communicate through words, facial expressions, the use of their eyes, gestures, and so on. The knowledge that you acquired in Stage 2 should help you here.

There's no need for you to change your feelings to match those of the majority; after all, if something doesn't amuse you, then it doesn't amuse you. But if you know that the majority will find a certain type of joke funny, then when people are laughing you can at least understand why. Having this skill will lessen your anxiety. It will also reduce the chances of you misunderstanding things you hear and help you choose your behavior so as to be better accepted. This stage, too, should also be approached with the help of a support person.

Stage 4: Have your first "trial run" in a small group

Accumulating knowledge will not raise your skill level all by itself. So after you've gone through Stages 2 and 3, it's time to practice what you've learned. This should be done in a small group where you feel safe and do not have to fear that you will be rejected if you make a mistake.

Here are two examples of groups where repeated trial and error will be easily accepted:

* groups, such as your social skills group or your buddy system that are intended for this type of practice

* groups made up of immediate or extended family members whom you can depend on for moral support.

Stage 5: Be selective in seizing opportunities for practice in more typical everyday settings

Just because you want to polish your skills and have some wisdom about how to do this, it does not follow that you're ready to practice in any situation. Sometimes, it's important to be able to deliberately forgo an opportunity to practice, perhaps because you're feeling low on mental or physical energy that day, or perhaps because the person who has invited you to join him or her is someone you do not feel comfortable interacting with.

Stage 6: Remember the importance of preparing before you practice

I recommend that you prepare before participating in social experiences in typical settings. For example, let's say you're planning to go to the movies with a group of classmates for the first time. If the place where you'll be meeting is outside of your neighborhood, then you should check in advance to find out how you might get to the meeting place. Is there a bus or a train you can take, will you have to arrange a lift in a car, or can you cycle or walk there? If this will be your first time going to a movie theater without an adult, then it might be a good idea to go with an adult first as a rehearsal. When you do this, pretend that you are by yourself and take charge of figuring out how to buy your ticket, where the toilet is, and so on. Also consider what you, personally, will want to do as an alternative if the movie you and your friends are planning to see is very popular and the seats are sold out at the time you go.

But preparation is nothing more than preparation. It is not uncommon for an actual situation to turn out differently from what you had imagined. So part of your preparation should include planning how to cope if something unexpected happens and you start to feel upset. For example, you can practice in advance so that under these circumstances you can try to relax by breathing deeply, or before leaving home you can attach a calming fidget item to your keychain.

SAMPLE STRATEGIES

To help you understand the principles involved in form-ulating special strategies and the procedures for practicing them, below I present three problem scenarios and possible ways of dealing with them. These scenarios all happen to deal with communication, but the same principles and procedures apply to other types of problems as well. Again, I recommend that you discuss with your support person the particular difficulties that you find yourself faced with in your own life. Chapter 5 provides additional examples.

Scenario 1: Telephone troubles

Some of the junior high school students I work with say that using the telephone causes them problems like the following: "It's hard to figure out what the person on the other end is saying, so I wind up asking them to repeat over and over." "I'm really uncomfortable asking people to repeat, so I hang up the phone without having really understood and am unable to pass along the message." "When I have to be spontaneous, I can't think of what to say, and I get really nervous."

Considering the characteristics of communication so often seen in people with AS, it is really no wonder that people on the autistic spectrum have trouble using the telephone effectively. Moreover, some individuals on the spectrum have distortions in their sense of hearing such that specific types of sound (such as the sound of certain voices when heard over the telephone) are especially difficult to perceive clearly. So what are some possible ways of dealing with all of this?

1. Let your immediate family members know that you have trouble understanding them when they try to tell you things by phone.

2. Turn on your answering machine and use it to screen calls. For example, you can decide only to pick up the phone if the caller is someone in your family.

3. Familiarize yourself with email and fax technologies, and use these options when practical.

4. Get special memo paper like the sample shown in the illustration and keep it right next to the phone, for times when you do pick it up. When you answer the phone, say, for example, "Hello, [your family name] residence..." Then if the family member being asked for is not home, use the memo paper to guide you as you take a message. For example, you can say: "Yes, I'll ask her to call you back as soon as she gets home. Please tell me your name and telephone number."

5. Write out a script of how you should begin and end
    a particular phone conversation and then try it out.
    For example, let's say it's evening and you want to
    ask a classmate a question. Your script might start
    like this: "Hello? This is [your name]. I'm in your
    son's class at school. I'm sorry for calling at this
    hour, but may I speak with
    him please?" And then
    for the ending, after your
    friend has given you
    the information you wanted:
    "Thanks a lot, [your
    friend's name]. Bye!"

6. Practice using the phone when you are feeling
    physically well and full of emotional energy, or with
    family members or other people you feel at ease
    with.

7. As you think about what career you might choose
    when you're older, favor options that will not involve
    a lot of telephone use.

Numbers 1 and 2 are examples of strategies that are well
matched to the situation of someone who is at the beginning
stage of dealing with telephone troubles. In other words, they
correspond to Stage 1 of the practice stages outlined earlier. If
you judge a certain strategy to be too difficult to work on
right now and think that attempting it will only end in failure,
then resolving to save it for some time in the future is a very
smart decision. Some people mistakenly believe that using
strategies like these to evade difficulties is a form of cheating,
but in fact avoiding unpleasantness and inconvenience is in
itself a worthwhile goal. The point is not that you should
avoid everything you find difficult. The point is rather that

you should set priorities. Have a discussion with your support person and, together, select the goal that makes sense to work on next.

Numbers 3, 4, and 5 are ways of complementing your traits, rather than trying to "fix" them (see Principle 2 on p.57). Numbers 4 and 5 also correspond to Stages 2, 5, and 6 (accumulating knowledge, selecting practice opportunities, and preparing in advance).

Number 6, which corresponds to Stage 5, represents the important skill of being able to judge when you are in the best condition for practicing a certain strategy. Finally, number 7 is about making life choices that genuinely suit you. The ability to do this is an important part of becoming your own support person.

Scenario 2: Misunderstanding people's words

Many people with AS have a strong preference for using words precisely. But in everyday life, words are often used in ways that are not reflected in dictionary definitions. Therefore, it is their very precision itself that can cause people with AS to get into trouble over the use of words.

One example of this phenomenon involves the use of the words, "I'm sorry." Consider the following hypothetical conversation:

Classmate: Ouch! If you're going to bump into someone, you should at least say "I'm sorry!"

You: But I didn't bump into you on purpose. Why should I apologize?!

It's true that dictionaries define "sorry" as an expression of apology or regret and define "apology" as, in part, an acknowledgment of fault. But in everyday life, people sometimes say "I'm sorry" even in situations that do not involve error, ill intent, or rudeness. In these situations, the expression is being used to verbally acknowledge that one has created a circumstance that has resulted in another person's having a bad experience. Here, the definition of "I'm sorry" can be stated like this: "I, too, think it is unfortunate that my action caused you unpleasantness." So in the above example, the boy who did the bumping should have said "I'm sorry" in order to express empathy with his classmate – i.e., to acknowledge that his classmate has experienced pain as a result of having been bumped and that this is unfortunate.

Just knowing the above can go a long way toward reducing problems related to the words "I'm sorry." Here, then, we have an example of Stage 2 (accumulating knowledge) being put into action. If you were to use this knowledge as background and next watch a TV soap opera or observe other children at school, chances are that you would eventually see similar exchanges that would cause you to think, "Aha! Now I get it!" At this point, you would be working on Stage 3 (observing and making inferences). Next, you could move on to Stages 4, 5, and 6 by practicing this new (for you) usage of the expression "I'm sorry" in appropriate situations.

Knowledge itself is not an automatic cure. To some extent, a characteristic of imagination in AS (difficulty making shifts in your mental state) is responsible for the inability to apologize the moment a situation arises where this is called for. Nevertheless, having this kind of knowledge puts you on the path toward less discomfort both for yourself and for the people you come into contact with.

Scenario 3: Misunderstanding body language

The potential for misunderstanding is not limited to spoken language, it extends even to eye contact, facial expressions, where people are standing and the direction they are facing, and so on.

I remember one consultation where the junior high school student I was to evaluate sat down with his elbows perched on the back of his chair and his back arched. His mother said, "That's rude!" to which he replied, "Huh? What's rude about sitting this way?" Do you know the answer to this boy's question?

Arching your back is a form of body language (a way of conveying emotions with your body) that conveys arrogance; it is used to show people that you are angry or that you consider them inferior. In the rules of communication used by the majority, there is almost always a one-to-one correspondence between this posture and the meaning of either arrogance or anger.

In the above example, I think that the boy had no intention whatsoever of trying to appear arrogant, rather he was simply making himself comfortable. Because he did not have any knowledge of what sort of impression this type of posture makes on most people, he was surprised when his mother scolded him.

My point is that studying the meanings of different forms of body language will serve you well by helping you to avoid being misunderstood and causing unpleasantness.

Some people with AS have poor control over the muscles needed to support the weight of their upper bodies; they tend to slump or have limbs that hang loosely. People like this have an easier time sitting still if they prop their elbows up on their chair backs. But even if the boy in my example above has this problem, knowing about body language gives him the opportunity to develop other strategies that might make things easier for him socially while still enabling him to sit comfortably.

Putting one's elbows on a chair's armrests is probably more socially acceptable than putting them on the chair's back. And someone with poor muscle control might be able to sit up straight without using his or her elbows, with intense concentration and the understanding that this would only be necessary for about three minutes. Or one might sit with elbows propped on the chair back but avert a mis-understanding by saying, "Please excuse my posture. Sitting this way really helps me to concentrate."

So, you see, even having poor posture does not have to interfere with alleviating difficulties in your everyday life. It all starts with knowledge (Stage 2).

What you learn about body language can then be applied to the challenge of making observations while watching television, which will further solidify your understanding (Stage 3). Moving on, you could then benefit from having other people tell you their impressions of your body language when you do a trial run in a small, safe group (Stage 4).

Again, whether we're considering body language or some other area of life, special strategies can help reduce problems and make your life easier and more pleasant!

CHAPTER 5

Hobbies – Five Major Trouble Spots

In this chapter, I use the example of hobby-related difficulties to explain the process of developing special strategies. The nature of problems faced and the most suitable strategies for dealing with them vary from one person to another, even among people who all have AS and therefore have similar brain types. Please work with your supporter to develop strategies that are appropriate for you.

People with AS have a large capacity for enjoying the world of hobbies, and it's wonderful to have a hobby that you enjoy. Not only do hobbies themselves enrich our lives, but they can also relieve us of the fatigue of dealing with people and increase our energy for coping with various life challenges.

We all have different hobbies. Trains, planes, computers, minerals, fossils, human anatomy, history, reading and writing…the list is endless. You may not be sure what your hobby is. But let's say that whenever you go shopping,

Wal-Mart stores are your place. Let's say that whenever the subject comes up, you tell people, "Discovering a new Wal-Mart makes me feel good; it's fun!" OK, so your hobby is…Wal-Mart! Some people love their studies or extra-curricular activities at school, and for them, these things are wonderful hobbies. In short, if it's something you want to keep learning more and more about, something you spend more time on than just about everyone else does or something that makes you feel happy or at ease just knowing about, then it's a hobby – and it's important to you.

So hobbies are important, but because you have AS, you probably tend to get overly enthusiastic about them, and this can cause you problems. Like these:

1. People get fed up and tell you, "Stop talking about the same thing all the time!"

2. You know when it's about time you should be turning your attention to other things, but you just can't make yourself stop.

3. You spend so much time on your hobby that you don't get around to finishing your homework.

4. You spend too much money on the hobby.

5. People tell you not to spend so much time off in your own world, or that you need to make more friends, and you start to feel unsure of yourself.

Let's talk about strategies for alleviating this kind of trouble.

PROBLEM 1: PEOPLE GET FED UP WITH YOU

"Stop talking about the same thing all the time!" It hurts your feelings when people say things like this, and the pain is even sharper when you stop and think that you've put them off. In addition, if people seem to be fed up with you over and over again, there's a danger that your relationships with those people will become more and more strained as time goes on.

So it's important to have a strategy that keeps people from feeling like you're always going on and on about the same thing and wanting to say to you, "Stop...!" The first step is learning how to answer the following questions correctly: With whom is it safe to talk about my hobby? When is it safe? And how much is safe? The key to deciding what's safe lies in understanding the different reasons people have for listening.

Why people might choose to listen when you talk about your hobby

When someone listens to you talking about your hobby, there are at least three possible reasons why:

1.   That person is actually also interested in the subject you're talking about.

2.   That person is interested in *you*. He or she cares
        about you and so wants to listen to anything you
        have to say.

3.   That person feels an obligation to listen to you
        because of his or her role in your life, or because the
        situation requires him or her to be polite.

If you can correctly determine which of these three reasons a
certain person has for listening to you, then it will be easier to
judge when it's OK to bring up the subject and for how long
it's OK to talk.

Example 1: If the person is a family member...

Imagine that you like ammonites (a kind of marine fossil).
Your family listens attentively when you talk about this hobby
and even goes with you to an ammonite museum. The most
likely reasons for their interest are these two:

1.   *They really like ammonites.*
        Lucky you! Actually, it's not uncommon for mothers
        or fathers to have the same hobby as their children –
        kindred spirits, right under the same roof.
            But be careful! In this situation, you and your
        like-minded parent need to have firm rules about
        how much time, space (for displays or storage), and
        money to spend on your hobby. Otherwise, you'll be
        making life very difficult for the other members of
        your family.

2.   *They care about you, so they want to hear about what
        interests you, and they enjoy seeing you happy.*
        Again, lucky you! You have a family that really values
        your importance. Even if they're not really interested
        in ammonites, there's nothing dishonest about their

behavior. They are acting out of genuine kindness toward you personally.

But be careful! Precisely because these are people you see every day, you need to respect their personal boundaries by asking them beforehand when it will be OK for you to talk, and for how long. This is a way of returning their kindness.

Example 2: If the person is a classmate...

Here, making a judgment gets very tricky, and not only because all three possibilities listed earlier must be considered. The really hard part is that the same classmate might have different reasons at different times. In one instance, he or she might listen because of a fondness for you (Reason 2), while at another time he or she might merely be tolerating your monologue out of a feeling of obligation (Reason 3).

Your classmate's reason for listening can change in a single instant. So what about the strategy of talking about your hobby while simultaneously trying to monitor the situation for sudden changes in your friend's attitude? I do not recommend this! For someone who has AS, this is an extremely difficult task, and trying it will defeat your purpose: instead of enjoying the time you spend talking about your hobby, you'll just wind up fatigued.

Remember, a classmate is someone you may feel embarrassed to make a social faux pas in front of (pressure!), and talking about your hobby is something that's very hard to stop once you get started. So using this particular situation to practice the skill of comprehending other people's reactions is not advantageous. Arrange to practice this skill at a different time, under safer circumstances. (For advice on this, see the discussion of stages for planning your learning experiences, beginning on p.59.)

You need other ideas. The following are three good ones.

Recommendation A: Find friends who really like ammonites

I highly recommend that you actively look for kindred spirits and then, as much as possible, talk about your hobby only with these people. But, unfortunately, the chances of finding people with the same hobby among your classmates are much slimmer than the chances of having a family member who shares your interest. Don't count on finding a fellow ammonite lover at school.

I think your best chance for success lies in joining a club or activities dedicated to your hobby. For example, you can participate in events sponsored by your local natural science museum, or by palaeontological societies. (Or, if you're a railway fan, you can join one of the many clubs devoted to this subject.)

When some students decide which high schools or colleges they want to apply to, they first find out whether or not the school has a club or classes related to their hobby. In contrast, some students decide that it's best to keep their hobby and school life separate, so instead they opt to look for a club outside of school. In either case, finding a place where you can give full expression to your interest is a good idea, and it has a double benefit: it not only raises the chances of finding people who share this hobby, but also makes the most of one of your positive AS traits – your great enthusiasm for a single subject.

Recommendation B: Be cautious about bringing up your hobby with people other than your club acquaintances or museum friends

If friends at school start talking about hobbies, then say something simple, such as "I like collecting fossils," and don't elaborate except to answer if someone asks you a question.

You may wish that it were possible to talk freely about your hobby with your classmates, since you spend time with them every day, and this feeling is only natural. But remember: the chance that someone in your class loves to talk about ammonites as much as you do is very, very small.

Recommendation C: Enjoy your hobby, and be proud of it!

The reason I suggest keeping quiet about your hobby under certain circumstances is simply to show you how to avoid unpleasantness for yourself. Your hobby is not something to be embarrassed about and does not need to be kept hidden. No matter how unusual your special interest is, you have nothing to be ashamed of – unless it involves possible harm to living creatures.* There can actually be benefits in letting friends, immediate family members, and other relatives know what your hobby is. For example, if they know that you like

---

*   If you feel yourself attracted to activities that involve harming living things, then you need to talk to your support person and let him or her help you find something else that captures your interest. It's important to have an ongoing hobby that will help you relax.

ammonites, they might send you information on the subject when they happen to come across some, or else bear your interest in mind if ever they're choosing a present to give you.

And, in my opinion, anyone who criticizes you solely because of the kind of hobby you have is not someone you should choose as a friend.

PROBLEM 2: YOU JUST CAN'T MAKE YOURSELF STOP

This is a problem I hear about very, very frequently, as people who have AS tend to get deeply absorbed. Special strategies are needed to help yourself stop working on your hobby when it's time to.

Recommendation A: Work on self-awareness

In other words, it's important to be aware that stopping is difficult for you. Having this awareness means, for example, that if you enjoy reading comic books you should not consider a plan where you decide, "I'll only read my comic book for five minutes; then I'll stop."

Recommendation B: Challenge your patience at the beginning, not the end

Once you realize that stopping is difficult for you, there are a number of strategies for compensating.

It's much easier to be patient and delay starting a favorite activity than it is to stop once you've started. For example, if there's a test you need to study for, then two effective strategies would be to:

1.   firmly decide that you will not buy a comic book today

2.   move any hobby-related temptations you can see around you out of sight.

When you do work on your hobby, work on it during one big chunk of time rather than in small bits and pieces. This way you can reduce the number of times you have to deal with the difficulty of stopping. For example, instead of opening a favorite book or getting on the internet several times in the same day, you'll do better by waiting until after all of your studying for the day is finished, or by waiting until the weekend, when you can enjoy a long, leisurely reading or websurfing session.

Recommendation C: Work on strategies for stopping

To practice stopping an activity you enjoy, try something like the following: Let's say you want to practice reading your comic book for one hour and then stop. In this case, start reading precisely one hour before a favorite television program comes on. What you're doing here is being aware of your difficulty and compensating for it by planning the activity so that there will be an easy stopping point. Look for these sorts of natural breaks that will help you make transitions from your hobby to other things. These natural breaks will also help you manage your study time.

You can also try setting a timer or asking your mother in advance to remind you when your prearranged stopping time has come.

But with this last strategy, it's important for both you and your mother not to get angry with each other! The purpose of her reminder is not to scold you, but rather to serve the same purpose as a bell or timer, with the added advantage that she can make sure that you've actually heard her. Moms, especially, please keep this crucial point in mind!

PROBLEM 3: YOUR HOBBY INTERFERES WITH YOUR HOMEWORK

Managing your time well is extremely important – and extremely difficult. This is because as a person with AS, you have an unusually strong capacity for getting deeply absorbed in activities that you enjoy. But by learning a few tricks for using time efficiently, you'll find that your life gets much easier. I highly recommend that you work on this issue with your support person (an adult who is on your side and in a position to help you; see Chapter 6) rather than trying to go it alone.

Recommendation: With your support person, practice the skills needed to budget your time

There are three procedures required to efficiently budget (i.e., manage) your time.

* *Procedure 1*: Keep track of when each homework assignment is due and of roughly how large each assignment is.

* *Procedure 2*: Keep track of when you will have time available, and how much.

* *Procedure 3*: Create a schedule.

In order to budget your time effectively, you need to make use of a number of skills, such as making predictions, simultaneously considering both the sum total of the tasks you have to complete and the time needed for each one, and making judgments about your own ability (estimating how much time you, personally, will need to complete your work).

None of these skills is easy for people with AS, but by enlisting a support person to help you practice, you will be able to master the process little by little.

Difficulty with time management is related to the characteristics not only of people with AS, but also of people with AD/HD. In the appendix to this book, I present a detailed method for budgeting time. Please refer to this section when practicing time management with your support person.

Please realize that there are many individuals with AS and AD/HD who live their lives without even being aware that there is such a thing in the world as "time management"! So even if you do not succeed right away, please understand that your determination to learn time-management skills is in itself a step forward.

PROBLEM 4: YOU SPEND TOO MUCH MONEY ON THE HOBBY

Money is not a serious problem while you're still young enough to be getting an allowance from your parents. Deep trouble can start, however, when you're older and are living by yourself and having to earn your own living.

The procedures for managing your money are similar to those for managing your time.

* *Procedure 1*: Determine how much money you have available.

* *Procedure 2*: Determine how much money you want to spend, including money you spend on a regular basis (such as for a weekly comic book).

* *Procedure 3*: Find a balance between what you want and what's available.

Until you reach adulthood, the pace of your monetary inflows and outgoings is likely to be irregular, with much of your money, for example, coming in the form of occasional gifts from relatives. And the amount of allowance money that parents give varies widely from one family to another.

If you've already found that you have trouble managing money, then it would be a good idea to start using the above procedures, enlisting the help of a support person for Procedure 3.

But if you're not having any specific problems with money right now, then it may be easier to work on these skills – again, with the help of a support person – when you're older and living on your own.

PROBLEM 5: YOU START TO FEEL UNSURE OF YOURSELF

When the adults in your life, or your classmates, say you should have more friends or be more tuned in to the people around you, it's easy to start having self-doubts. But unlike the inability to manage time and money, which is a genuine problem, the ability to get "carried away" with a hobby is actually a good thing. Don't be put off by what other people say.

Certainly, there are people with AS who themselves are worried or feel hurt because they're unable to make friends. This is only natural, since AS is defined by the triad characteristics, which include having an unusual way of interacting with people. Let's talk a bit about what we mean by the word "friend." Please work with a support person as you think about these issues.

Having friends

Some of you may watch classmates laughing together and wish you could take part in the same kind of enjoyment. But consider the social conventions of people in the majority: it is customary for friends to listen to each other talk about their hobbies even when they're not really interested. For example, if you expect friends to give you enthusiastic attention when you talk about ammonites, then you need to reciprocate by also listening enthusiastically when your friends are talking about their favorite TV soap opera, even if you actually couldn't care less. In other words, having friends in the conventional sense means participating in a group and going with the flow of changes in other people's feelings and wishes. And getting friends to join you in what you want to do means that you must also be willing to change your plans to join them when they ask you to.

Is all of this really what you want?

There are lots of things about the social conventions of the majority that just don't suit the AS way of being. So it's important to think about how to have friendships on your own terms.

Don't be swayed by the idea of "the more, the merrier"

It's generally understood that adults have only a limited amount of time and energy to spend on socializing with friends, given the commitments posed by work, family, and activities done for the sake of self-improvement. Adults with lots of friends get complimented for being "good at networking," "a people person," and so on, but adults who don't have lots of friends get compliments, too, for "making time with their families a high priority" or for "being careful to safeguard their own private time." It's not as though one of these ways of being is wonderful and the other is something to be ashamed of.

So why is it that children are constantly being told, and made to think, that having lots of friends is such a great thing? Personally, I don't understand it. It's impossible to become "friends," in the true sense of the word, with every single one of your classmates. Moreover, it's unnecessary. Of course, it's important that you be able to get along, and developing strategies for doing so is something you need to work on with your support person.

Which situation is more personally satisfying – having a hundred friends with whom you share a variety of everyday interests in a superficial way, or having only one friend with whom you deeply share your hobby – i.e., your most valued interest? The answer to this question is different for different people.

In fact, there are even people who, although they interact with others as necessary in their everyday lives, do not desire to have actual friends and nevertheless lead perfectly satisfying lives.

It's not a matter of good or bad; if you're being true to yourself, then you're doing fine.

The nature of childhood

It's generally assumed that your "friends" are the children you share hobbies with, and go to school with, and go places with on the weekends. But is this necessarily so?

Most adults, for example, wouldn't go to the movies with a person they worked with. Similarly, it would be extremely rare for a group of people who work at the same company to decide to go on vacation together as individuals. This is simply because it's unusual for people to have jobs, hobbies, and lifestyles all in common. So for most people, work is work, hobbies are hobbies, and home life is home life – and social relationships are compartmentalized accordingly.

So why is it that in the world of children, friends so often do everything together? What is the seeming mystery that puts children with the same interests and lifestyles together in the same class at the same school?

The answer is that most children have not yet developed specialized interests and habits. In the case of hobbies, for example, many have not been lucky enough to find one that truly fascinates them, or else their ability to become fascinated is still weak. This is why they are able to show some interest in each other's hobbies and activities. Of course, we can express this in a positive way by saying that they are highly flexible. Just like AS characteristics, non-AS characteristics also can be seen as having both advantages and disadvantages.

To put it bluntly, many children with AS have already achieved an adult level of specialization, and yet they are expected to live at a much lower level of maturity.

Recommendation A: Compartmentalize your relationships

I think that maintaining relationships with different people for different purposes is an especially good idea for people who have AS. For example, I suggest that you spend time studying with your classmates, have fun with the other people in your special interest club, and go places with your immediate family (or other relatives). I know I'm repeating myself, but it's just very unlikely that you'll find someone you can share your hobby with in the typical group of children your age, most of whom do not have highly specialized interests.

One advantage of this approach to relationships is that it's easy to understand how you should act, what your role is, and where the limits are in a given social situation. If you know that a certain person is your "ammonite friend," then you can relax and plunge right into the world of marine fossils the minute you see each other, without the need for a preface or small talk.

Please understand that these compartmentalized relationships are in no way inferior to the more common "do-it-all" friendships. But also be aware that these relationships can sometimes evolve: You may find that the scope of your friendship with a certain individual broadens over time at a speed and to a degree that seem mutually comfortable. This is OK, too.

Recommendation B: Spend time with people who are capable of appreciating the good things about AS

The positive aspects of AS are very difficult for children to understand. For you, therefore, friendships may have to wait until you are older and have more opportunities to let your interests flourish. Don't hurry; wait until you meet someone who truly understands your worth. Someone who sidles up to you and says "OK, I'll be your friend" probably isn't!

Another frequent assumption is that friends are supposed to be the same age. This, too, is just not so. There are children with AS who form hobby-based friendships that are mutually satisfying with people much older than they are. And some children enjoy wonderful and irreplaceable relationships with their grandparents. It may be that precisely because you have AS, you are able to remain free from confining assumptions about social hierarchy and build relationships with people regardless of age. It also seems to me that people with AS have a special knack for making others feel this same kind of freedom. It would be a shame to let yourself be trapped by the idea that you need to make friends who are the same age as you.

Recommendation C: Get to know other people with AS

At the clinic where I work, we have experimental groups for people with AS. Many of the children in these groups say things like, "I felt right at ease here from the very beginning," "People here seem to talk at the right pace for me," and "We can all understand what the others have been through." Of course, the fact that two people have AS is not a guarantee that they will like each other, but it does seem that the chances of this happening are higher.

If you have an opportunity to meet in person with others who have AS, you will get a much stronger sense that you are not alone in having this set of characteristics. You will also be able to see that there is great variety even among the AS population. In other words, you may share the same AS traits with others, but AS by itself does not define your personhood.

And so I recommend that you try getting together with others who have AS, if ever an opportunity presents itself. This is another good thing to discuss with your support person. Even if there is no practical way for you to meet other children with AS, your support person may be able to help you find adults who can tell you about children they know who have it, or help you find memoirs written by people who have it. Listening to or reading these personal stories should also prove helpful to you.

Recommendation D: Work on polishing the skill of spending time alone

Many people with AS are especially good at spending time alone. Yet any skill needs polishing in order for it to continue to shine.

For example, some people with AS do not find it quite enough to enjoy their hobbies all by themselves; they like to constantly have family members or others watching and listening. A hobby is something special that can be enjoyed throughout your entire life, but if you feel like you need an audience, then this enjoyment can be dampened or spoiled. Of course, it is nice to have people see and hear about your accomplishments. But – again taking the example of ammonites – the real definition of success is what happens between you and the fossils and how much your world as an individual is enriched as a result. So even though you were born with autistic spectrum characteristics, you still need to make a conscious effort to develop your capacity to enjoy the world of hobbies solo.

I also suggest that you work on your skills for passing time alone at school. There's no shame whatsoever in using your recess time to relax by reading a book or just resting. In contrast, this is just one more example of using your time in a way that takes advantage of your positive AS traits. Anyone who criticizes you for doing so – even if that person happens to be your homeroom teacher – just doesn't fully understand the good things about AS.

If you are going through a stage where you've lost confidence in yourself and have made it your life's goal to appear as though you belong to the majority, then you might have trouble accepting my advice, which is intended to encourage you to be yourself. But remember the results of brain research presented in Chapter 1. There is nothing mistaken in the way you feel about things. And you are not a counterfeit human being! You just happen to be a minority member of the population of planet earth.

You are a real, OK person who happens to have AS.

CHAPTER 6

Support and Understanding

WHOM SHOULD YOU TELL ABOUT YOUR AS?

You know that you have an autistic spectrum condition – a type of brain that places you in the minority. AS is not a bad thing, and it is nothing to be ashamed of. But does this mean that when meeting people for the first time, you should introduce yourself by saying, "Hello, my name is so-and-so. I have Asperger syndrome"?

I don't think so.

Being on the autistic spectrum is a very special and important fact about you. I recommend that you generally keep important information like this private and only reveal it to people who will understand its importance and treat it with appropriate care and respect.

Asperger syndrome is not yet widely understood. Some people, therefore, might have misconceptions about you or harbor malicious intent toward you if they were to learn that you've been diagnosed with AS. This would be very distressing for you, and even if it did not occur, you would still have the heavy burden of frequently being asked to explain about AS and having to answer people's questions.

But it is also true that sometimes only talking openly with people around you can make you feel understood and put you at ease. It's difficult to spend all of your days without being able to talk to anyone about something so deeply personal.

I suggest that you discuss with your support person which people you can safely tell about your AS and how much information you should share with them.

I also think it's a good idea to let your support person help you explain about your AS to the other people in your life that you've decided to tell. Specifically:

★ Your support person can be the one who tells your homeroom teacher.

★ Your homeroom teacher can be given information and taught skills that will enable him or her to become an additional support person for you, and he or she can then be the one who tells your classmates that you have AS, if you have decided to let them know.

★ Alternatively, you and your support person can work together to prepare a written explanation about your AS and then you yourself can recite this explanation to your class.

I know that you already understand this, but just to remind you: the reason for being cautious and not telling anyone and everyone you have AS is not because you have something to be ashamed of. The reason is that your having AS is important information, and you deserve to have it used in the best way possible.

KNOWING WHO TO ASK FOR SUPPORT

Each human being is unique. Therefore, no one coping strategy can be a perfect fit for everyone, even for a group of people who have the same AS traits. This is because having AS is only part of who you are. No matter what strategy you use, it will have to be fine-tuned – i.e., adjusted – to suit your disposition, living environment, family history, and so on. Your efforts will be most effective if you enlist the help of an adult for this kind of fine-tuning. Seeking out and finding an adult to assist you in this way is one of the most important things you can do to make the most of your life.

What is a "support person"?

A support person is an adult who works with you to consider what strategies to use in order to bring out the best in yourself. This person, of course, must be someone you feel safe and at ease talking with about personal matters.

Talking things over with a support person will help you think of more ideas than you would all by yourself. It will also make it easier for you to figure out what went wrong if you try an idea that does not work. And, most important of all, just knowing that there is someone on your side will give you courage.

Support people within the family

It's very important to have a support person in your immediate family. Not having anyone at home who truly understands you is highly distressing psychologically and can also make your everyday life much more difficult. Remember that your mother, father, or both were the ones whose planning and arrangements made it possible for your AS to be discovered in the first place; consider them good candidates for the job of support person. There should be someone in your family you can turn to for help.

You might be thinking, "But my mother (father) is always nagging or criticizing me, so we always end up arguing." If so, please realize that she (or he) needs to go through a process of learning how to be your support person, just as you need to go through the process of learning to deal with your AS.

You and your support person (or people) form a team. When something is not going well between you, work together on looking for a better way rather than blaming each other. This is called being a "team player."

Professional support people

Ideally, you should also have one or more support people outside of your immediate family – for at least two reasons. First, if you have any worries about your relationship with one or both of your parents, it will be easier to talk these over with a person outside of the family. Second, a professional can offer you an additional perspective on any given problem.

The professional who first explained to you about your having AS (whether he or she was a doctor, a psychologist, or some kind of therapist) should of course be considered as a possible support person. Your homeroom teacher at school and your school's guidance counselor are also in positions where they should be able to offer you support. But, unfortunately, the key word here is "should." The reality is that understanding of AS is still inadequate, so the people who should be helping you often don't have the knowledge or skills to do so; in some cases, they may also be too busy to talk with you. I recommend that you talk with your in-family support person – i.e., your mother or father – about who might make a good support person outside of the family.

IF YOU ARE USING THIS BOOK ON YOUR OWN

Some of you reading this book may have found it on your own, in the process of working by yourself to deal with personal characteristics that you find troubling or troublesome. Some of you may even be adults who no longer live with your parents.

Unfortunately, there isn't any one place that I can refer you to where you are absolutely guaranteed to find an appropriate support person. But don't give up! The fact that you were able to find this book solely through your own efforts means that you are very resourceful and will surely be able to find a support person – someone who can give you understanding and help you with strategies – as well.

If you are not yet an adult

If you are not yet an adult, I recommend that you talk over the ideas in this book with your parents. Most likely, your parents know a lot less about AS than you do. They might misunderstand you when you try to explain, or they might even scold you for wanting to learn about AS in the first place. But don't get angry, and don't give up. It may just be the suddenness of the new information that has them upset or angry.

First, try giving them this book. Next, tell them that you would like to consult a professional. Trying to determine by yourself whether or not you have an "AS brain" is very difficult and potentially dangerous.

In order to arrange for you to consult a professional, your parents should read the next section for those who are adults. This explains how a referral may be organized. The procedures are the same whether they are followed by your parents or by you for yourself.

If you are an adult

If you are an adult and are in a situation where you cannot discuss with your parents the possibility that you have AS, or feel very reluctant to do so, then I suggest that you should try to obtain professional help for yourself.

In the US

If you live in the United States, an advisable first step is to contact the Autism Society of America. The website of the Autism Society features an online resource directory, Autism Source, which allows for a search of professionals by geographic location. It will be most helpful to determine whether or not a subchapter of the Autism Society exists in your city or state. Contacting a local organization will provide access to more extensive information about resources in your area; there are, as yet, few professionals specializing in the diagnosis of AS in adults. The Autism Society also hosts internet message boards on which one can post requests for referrals in your vicinity. Diagnostic evaluations should be administered by a psychologist or psychiatrist, and it is often advisable to be evaluated by a multidisciplinary team with professionals from other disciplines, such as speech and language pathology or social work. It is essential that the diagnostic assessment be administered by professionals experienced in assessing individuals with autism spectrum disorders, as distinguishing among AS and other psychiatric or language disorders in adulthood can be difficult.

Many diagnosticians do not accept insurance. You should contact the provider to determine whether your insurance is accepted and, if not, the cost of the evaluation. If insurance is accepted, your health plan may require you to obtain an official referral from your primary care physician. Some health plans may require you to visit professionals within a specific network; it remains essential for you to seek out a professional with experience diagnosing autism spectrum disorders in adults. Unfortunately, specialists often have long waiting lists. Contacting a local support group or joining an online message board can offer valuable support during the interim.

Autism Society of America
7910 Woodmont Avenue, Suite 300
Bethesda, MD 20814–3067, USA
Tel: 301 657 0881 or 1 800 3AUTISM (1 800 328 8476)
www.autism-society.org

The Autism Society of America (ASA) works to increase public awareness about the day-to-day issues faced by those with autism and their families and provides information and education about autism. There are local chapters throughout the United States.

In the UK

If you live in the UK, the first step is to contact the National Autistic Society's (NAS) helpline to find out what diagnostic and support services are available near to where you live. As yet there are only a small number of centers that work with adults. These may be run by psychologists or psychiatrists or both, often working with speech and language therapists and social workers. The professionals involved have to have a special interest in autistic spectrum disorders, including AS, and special training in diagnosis and ways of helping. There are also a few professionals who work on their own. Some of these services are within the National Health Service (NHS) and therefore are free to people in their area. However, others are run by charities or privately and have to charge fees. Some NHS centers will see people from outside their areas but charge fees for this. Your local NHS Primary Care Trust (PCT) has to agree to pay the fees for you.

The NAS helpline will tell you how to contact the centers nearest to you. For some, you can make contact directly. For others, including those under the NHS, you will have to see your general practitioner (GP). In some areas, your GP can refer you to a specialist center. In other areas, your GP has to refer you to a local consultant psychiatrist. If the local psychiatrist agrees that you need to be seen at a specialist centre, they can make the referral and, if necessary, ask for any fees to be paid by the NHS PCT. You can ask the NAS helpline staff to send you a copy of the leaflet called "Gaining a Diagnosis in Adulthood" and another called "Why Get a Diagnosis as an Adult?", both of which contain information you will find useful. You should also ask for "A GP's Guide to Adults with Asperger's Syndrome" to give to your doctor. This helps to explain to your GP why you want to be referred to a specialist centre for diagnosis and support.

Unhappily, there is no certainty that you will be able to be seen at a specialist center. If you cannot be referred and cannot refer yourself, you should contact the NAS again or your local Autistic Society to find out what help there is available. The

NAS helpline can give you details of your local Autistic Society.

In order to arrange for you to consult a professional, your parents should read the next section for those who are adults. This explains how a referral may be organised. The procedures are the same whether they are followed by your parents or by you for yourself.

The National Autistic Society
393 City Road
London EC1V 1NG, UK
Tel: 020 7833 2299
Fax: 020 7833 9666
Email: nas@nas.org.uk
www.nas.org.uk

The National Autistic Society (NAS) aims to help people with autism in the UK by ensuring the quality of needed services provided for them and their families. There are local chapters throughout England, Scotland, Wales and Northern Ireland.

In Australia

If you live in the Australia, the first step is to contact your local Autism Spectrum Association to find out what diagnostic and support services are available near to where you live. Each state provides different services and can direct you to a range of local professionals and support services. The professionals involved have to have a special interest in autistic spectrum disorders, including Asperger syndrome, and special training in diagnosis and ways of helping. There are also a few professionals who work on their own; Tony Attwood's clinic "Hearts and Minds" in Brisbane is the most well-known in Australia, and there are a range of other private professionals in most states. Please we aware that in most cases there are waiting lists for diagnosis, and it can be a lengthy process.

For family members, partners or parents of people who they suspect have AS, it can be very difficult to raise the topic. Once again it is definitely worth calling your local Autism Spectrum Association to ask for guidance and support.

Autism Council of Australia Ltd
PO Box 361, Forestville, NSW 2087
Australia
Tel: 02 8977 8300
Fax: 02 8977 8399
www.autismaus.com.au

The Autism Council of Australia Ltd (ACA) focuses on working with governments to develop policies for those who have autism and their families and carers, and their website has links to all autism spectrum associations.

How to ask questions when seeking information

Many staff in information and consultation centers are not trained to deal with telephone inquiries from individuals who themselves have AS. I therefore suggest that if your support person is someone who lives with you, then you should ask that person to call for information on your behalf.

If your situation is such that you are truly grappling with your concerns alone and there is no one but yourself to make the call, then I recommend that you begin the conversation by stating clearly: "I'm calling because I think I have Asperger syndrome." Further, I recommend that you use this first telephone call only to explain that you wish to send an email message or fax describing the details of your situation. Sending the details in writing will result in less possibility of misunderstandings, and it will also give the people at the organization a chance to prepare a thorough response.

A Message to the Reader – You Are a Wonderful and Caring Person!

There was this time when I was speaking to a group of elementary school children who all had AS, and I showed them a treasured heirloom of mine. "This," I explained, "is a book given to me 35 years ago by my uncle, whom I loved very much." Then I continued by inviting the children to ask me questions. Inwardly, I was expecting that they would ask about my uncle.

But instead, I got questions like these: "What is the point size of the type used in the book?" and "How many pages are there?"

That's the way it goes, I suppose. Asking about the doctor's beloved uncle would have been the first priority for the majority population. Being interested in the book as a book, and moreover as an antique, and wondering about type sizes and page numbers were the top priorities in this group of children representing a minority population – though I must add that not everyone with AS would necessarily have the same sort of questions. Please understand: I do not believe that in a situation like this, you're "supposed to" show an interest in the uncle first. After all, the human heart is free. But I do believe that it can be advantageous for people with AS to be aware of what tends to interest the majority in various situations, including this one.

People with AS are sometimes told they are lacking in common sense. But what's called common sense is dictated by the perspective of the majority, and to people with AS it can sometimes seem illogical. You may wonder, for example, why it is never OK under any circumstances to pass food, such as a bread roll, to someone by throwing it, even though this method might get the food to the other person faster and also might mean that you don't have to stand up and walk across the room. Or why you get scolded for not looking at people when they're talking to you, even though you have trouble concentrating when you're making eye contact and can actually understand them better by standing sideways and turning your ear toward their faces. Many children with AS ask me about problems like this, and many also berate themselves, sometimes sadly and sometimes in anger, saying that they "must be hopelessly lacking in common sense" because they have questions like these.

In response to such questions, have you ever been given advice similar to the following? Sure, passing food to someone by throwing it may be efficient, but the majority of people will think this looks too much like you're feeding a zoo animal and will therefore mistakenly believe you're deliberately being rude. This is why it's not a good idea. And it's wonderful that you've discovered you can concentrate better when someone is talking if you stand so as to avoid making eye contact, but the majority of people will mistake this posture to mean that you're not interested in listening to them or that you don't like them. So if you do want to do this, you should first explain to the other person, "Please excuse my manners, but I have an easier time listening when my ear is turned toward people."

Please understand that having needed to hear advice like this does not make you "hopeless" and is no reason to feel bad about yourself!

By this point in your life, you've probably been given lots of advice from all kinds of people – family, teachers, professionals at clinics you may have attended and so on. The reason for the kind of advice you get at these places is not that there's anything wrong with the way you think, or your personal perspective on things. If these professionals were to voice the real reason, it would be something like this: "We see the truth of your thoughts and your perspective, but we are asking you to acquire the skill of adjusting to the logic of the majority, because this will make life easier both for you and for everyone else."

I, for one, deeply appreciate the constant efforts that you make to adjust to the majority way of doing things.

When you were little, it was your mother's and father's job to help you find your strengths and to protect you from having too many sad experiences as a result of things you found difficult. But now you've grown to an age where your parents cannot always be there for you.

Your mother, father, and all the other grownups who care about you would like you to have skills you can use to help yourself as you go through life. They want you to discover habits and strategies that work for you and to hold your head high and use them proudly. They want you to eventually become your own number-one support person so you can cheer yourself on. They trust in your ability to do this, because they've seen how hard and earnestly you've worked to learn the majority way of doing things. They know what a wonderful and caring person you are.

A Message to Support People

THIS BOOK IS NOT A DIAGNOSTIC MANUAL!

The information presented in Part 1 of this book should help parents and teachers to understand the characteristics of AS. But it is not meant to be a comprehensive treatise. In fact, explanations of certain behavioral characteristics – those regarding which children are unlikely to have self-awareness – have been deliberately omitted. I encourage you to make use of some of the selections on the recommended reading list at the back of this book to help you, as a support person, deepen your understanding of the issues faced by the children you are involved with.

In addition, if a child believes himself or herself to fit the descriptions in this book, please be aware that it is dangerous to jump to the conclusion that he or she has AS just on this basis alone. There is always the chance that the similarities that the child identifies with are actually symptoms of a psychiatric illness unrelated to any developmental disorder. A diagnosis cannot be made without a professional evaluation.

ADJUSTING THE CHILD'S ENVIRONMENT IS AN IMPORTANT FORM OF SUPPORT

I have included in this book only information that I deemed to be appropriate for use specifically by children who have AS. For this reason, the scope of this book is not sufficient to provide support people with all of the background they need to fulfill their role.

The most important omission is information concerning techniques for adjusting the child's environment. If children who have AS are expected to coexist successfully with what I call "the majority" – i.e., the more typical individuals they are surrounded by in their everyday lives – on the strength of sheer effort and raised awareness alone, then it is very unlikely that they will be able to do so without losing their self-confidence and pride. Much understanding and finesse is also needed on the part of everyone in the child's life.

Encouraging people in the majority to develop this kind of sensitivity requires a good deal of social know-how. This is a burden that should not be placed on the individuals for whom this book was primarily written – i.e., children who themselves have AS. If these children themselves were to ask for adjustments in their environment in ways that others found difficult to accept, then they would be opening them-selves up to entirely misguided criticisms of being selfish or defiant, or of using their diagnosis as an excuse.

I am trusting that you, the adult support person who has undertaken to read this book, have the determination to shoulder this important burden on behalf of the child you are trying to help. But you will need knowledge and skill, so I encourage you to continue learning as much as you can about techniques for supporting people on the autistic spectrum (individuals with Asperger syndrome or autism). I think it is important that you yourself find someone to consult with. The section in Chapter 6 entitled "If you are an adult" (p.94) should prove useful to you in this endeavor.

SUPPORT PEOPLE CAN HELP TAILOR GENERAL ADVICE TO SUIT THE INDIVIDUAL

Depending on the individual child's particular circumstances, even a strategy that is generally appropriate for children who have AS has the potential actually to make things worse. I have tried to be very careful in this book to discourage children from adopting plans that do not fit their own situations.

To maintain children's interest and make the subject easier to understand, I have included a number of concrete examples in the advice section of the book. At the same time, however, I have repeatedly reminded readers that they need to fine-tune each strategy with the help of a support person in order to render it appropriate to their own individual characteristics and situation.

Getting the most out of this book requires taking a close look at the individual child's current circumstances and skill levels and then using this as a basis for determining what the most appropriate goal is for that child to be working on right now. Giving a child effective support entails offering concrete advice that is tailor-made to suit that child as an individual.

I am placing my trust in you, who have chosen to take on the role of support person, to carry out this important work.

ALONG WITH TEACHING SKILLS, ALSO TEACH PRIDE IN MAKING USE OF THOSE SKILLS

At the clinic where I practice, we now place great emphasis on teaching children themselves psychological principles. The necessity of doing so was impressed upon us during our earlier work with children, and we have only just begun to grapple with it.

Children with high-functioning autism and Asperger syndrome can learn a great many skills with special educational guidance. At one time, I worked in a public therapy center in the city of Yokohama where the system of autism-related interventions available was particularly rich. Even high-functioning children were given access to support from kindergarten age or earlier. Because of all the skills they acquired at this stage, many of them adapted so well during the early years of elementary school that they seemed not to have any problems at all. And so it was thought that if only we could provide them with still more skills, we would be handing them the keys to happiness. Of course, having skills is a good thing, and not ensuring that children have the opportunity to acquire them is a grave problem. But we must also realize that teaching skills alone is not enough, for it does not foster in children the ability to live their lives with a sense of pride.

Remember, for a moment, the third-grade girl mentioned on p.55. Every time she employed the skill of saying only the second thing that came into her mind, she was devaluing herself.

Along with teaching skills, we must also teach pride in making use of those skills. Both skill and pride are intimately related, but they are not identical, and each must be consciously and separately taught. While the second is of course difficult to achieve without the first, having the first does not automatically guarantee the second.

With this in mind, we at our clinic have embarked on educating children about AS and related psychological issues. One manifestation of this approach is our series of workshops for junior high school students. The teaching materials I developed for those classes have formed the basis for this book.

It is my fervent hope that this book will help children to be themselves, and to do so with pride.

Recommended Reading

The Complete Guide to Asperger's Syndrome by Tony Attwood, London: Jessica Kingsley Publishers, 2007.

The Autistic Spectrum: A Guide for Parents and Professionals by Lorna Wing, London: Constable and Robinson, 2003.

A Guide to Asperger Syndrome by Christopher Gillberg, Cambridge: Cambridge University Press, 2002.

Parent's Guide to Asperger Syndrome and High-functioning Autism: How to Meet the Challenges and Help Your Child Thrive by Sally Ozonoff, Geraldine Dawson, and James McPartland, New York: The Guilford Press, 2002.

Autism and Asperger Syndrome – Preparing for Adulthood by Patricia Howlin, London: Routledge, 2004.

Appendix: Steps for Effective Time Management

People who have the characteristics of AS or AD/HD tend to have great difficulty budgeting their time effectively. I recommend that you work with a support person on developing your time-management skills, using the procedures outlined below as a guide.

PROCEDURE 1: KEEP TRACK OF HOMEWORK

The steps below will help you keep track of homework. First, the basics:

★ *Step 1*: Get a calendar or planner that allows you to view one full month at a time (see illustration).

* *Step 2*: Write *all work* related to your studies in this calendar – everything, including regular school homework, "cram school" homework, and tests you need to prepare for. When you are told about a test or homework assignment while at school, write this information down immediately on memo paper or in some other appropriate place. When you get home that day, copy this information into your monthly calendar (planner).

* *Step 3*: Make sure to write assignments down under the due date – not under the date on which you were told about them!

If you follow these three steps, then you will be able to keep track of your assignments without forgetting about them. And just by opening up your calendar, you'll be able to see your homework schedule for the month at a single glance. This will help you grasp the full volume of the work you need to do. And, in turn, grasping this will put you well on your way to being a person who can plan ahead!

Next, let's take this procedure to a higher level. I recommend that you start working on Step 4 only after you've gotten used to Steps 1–3.

* *Step 4*: Sometimes, the work for an assignment needs to be divided into separate stages. In this case, write each stage down separately in your calendar (planner) under appropriate dates. This will save you from having to do all of the work in a mad rush right before the due date.

Here's an example taken from the calendar of a junior high school student. This student's class has an English quiz every Friday, but of course there is also other work to be managed, as when the student's social studies teacher gives the following assignment: "Interview your family members on their thoughts about the ecology and write a report discussing their responses and what you have learned in your own research." The due date for this project is June 18 (Friday).

The student decides to do the interviewing on Sunday, since that is the easiest time to talk to his family members when they're not too busy. He selects Wednesday as the day to do research, because school lets out early that day, and tentatively decides to write the report on that day as well if possible. This plan will enable him to study for his English quiz on Thursday without feeling rushed. Here's how he might write this schedule in his calendar:

June 13: Social studies – interview family

June 16: Social studies – research

June 17: Social studies – extra day (just in case) to write report if needed

June 18: Social studies – hand in ecology report

PROCEDURE 2: KEEP TRACK OF AVAILABLE TIME

Divide the time you usually spend at home into the following three segments and then try plotting your weekly routine on a graph and see how it looks:

* routine activities (eating, bathing, etc.)

* sleep

* "free" time (available for studies and hobbies).

You will be using this time-management graph and the calendar (planner) filled in based on Procedure 1 to create a detailed time schedule.

Routine activities and sleep generally require about the same number of hours each day. And you can also take account of the number of hours on any given day that you will be spending in class, at after-school extracurricular activities, or at "cram school." For example, you can say that "On Wednesdays, I have two hours free before dinner and three hours afterward," or "On Thursdays, I go to 'cram school,' which leaves me with only one hour free..." This is what I mean by determining your available time on a daily basis. Your time-management graph need be made only once, as it can be photocopied, transferred to a whiteboard imprinted with a weekly schedule chart (see illustration), or input into your computer.

PROCEDURE 3: CREATE A SCHEDULE

First, you need to think about what time of day to set aside for homework. In other words, each day when you get home from school, you need to decide how to divide your time between studying and leisure (working on your hobby or watching TV).

By looking at your calendar (planner), you'll be able to remember what you absolutely need to do that day for homework. And by looking at your graph, you'll be able to see where in your afternoon and evening there is time available – and how much time there is.

Now you're ready to decide exactly when today you will do your homework. Instead of just making the decision in your head, mark it down on your graph. This way, the schedule you worked so hard to create will not be forgotten, and you will be even more motivated to follow it. The illustration below shows an example where study time has been plotted on the graph using magnets.

Procedure 3 can be completed in about three minutes, as long as your calendar is already filled in and your graph is made.

If you create a schedule where you plan on studying after working on your beloved hobby, there's a danger that you will find making the transition too difficult. People with AS have a very hard time stopping something once they've started. To create a schedule that's as practical as possible, refer to the advice on p.79.

As you practice managing your time, keep the three procedures at the forefront of your mind. When you first start, you may have trouble planning your time well or doing things according to the schedule you created, but if you consciously apply all of the steps in the correct order and work with a support person, then your skills will gradually improve.

In contrast, if you ignore the three procedures and instead just make a plan haphazardly and then try to learn from what went wrong, your efforts will be less effective.

References

Asperger, H. (1944 [1991]) " 'Autistic Psychotherapy' in childhood." (transl. U. Frith) In: U. Frith (ed.) *Autism and Asperger Syndrome.* Cambridge: Cambridge University Press.

Baron-Cohen, S., Ring, H.A., Wheelwright, S., Bullmore, E.T., *et al.* (1999) "Social intelligence in the normal and autistic brain: An fMRI study." *European Journal of Neuroscience 11,* 6, 1891–1898.

Gillberg, C. (2002) *A Guide to Asperger Syndrome.* Cambridge: Cambridge University Press.

Schultz, R.T., Gauthier, I., Klin, A., Fulbright, R.K., *et al.* (2000) "Abnormal ventral temporal cortical activity during face discrimination among individuals with autism and Asperger syndrome." *Archives of General Psychiatry 57,* 4, 331–340.

Yoshida, Y. and Uchiyama, T. (2004) "The clinical necessity for assessing AD/HD symptoms in children with high-functioning PDD." *European Child and Adolescent Psychiatry 13,* 5, 307–314.